Computer Science, Technology and Applications

Computer Science, Technology and Applications

Emerging Applications of Blockchain Technology
Vinod Kumar Shukla, PhD (Editor)
Sonali Vyas, PhD (Editor)
Shaurya Gupta, PhD (Editor)
Suchi Dubey, PhD (Editor)
2023. ISBN: 979-8-89113-101-9 (Hardcover)
2023. ISBN: 979-8-89113-185-9 (eBook)

Digital Transformation – Modernization and Optimization of Wireless Networks
Ram Krishan, PhD (Editor)
Manpreet Kaur, PhD (Editor)
Jagtar Singh, PhD (Editor)
Shilpa Mehta, PhD (Editor)
Vikas Goyal (Editor)
2023. ISBN: 979-8-89113-042-5 (Softcover)
2023. ISBN: 979-8-89113-116-3 (eBook)

Digital Twins: The Industry 4.0 Use Cases: The Technologies, Tools, Platforms and Application
Kavita Saini, PhD (Editor)
Pethuru Raj Chelliah, PhD (Editor)
2023. ISBN: 979-8-89113-057-9 (eBook)

Situational Modeling: Definitions, Awareness, Simulation
Alexander Fridman, PhD (Editor)
2023. ISBN: 979-8-88697-590-1 (Hardcover)
2023. ISBN: 979-8-88697-725-7 (eBook)

More information about this series can be found at
https://novapublishers.com/product-category/series/computer-science-technology-and-applications/

Manaswini Pradhan
and Satchidananda Dehurl
Editors

Information and Knowledge Systems

Copyright © 2024 by Nova Science Publishers, Inc.

All rights reserved. No part of this book may be reproduced, stored in a retrieval system or transmitted in any form or by any means: electronic, electrostatic, magnetic, tape, mechanical photocopying, recording or otherwise without the written permission of the Publisher.

We have partnered with Copyright Clearance Center to make it easy for you to obtain permissions to reuse content from this publication. Please visit copyright.com and search by Title, ISBN, or ISSN.

For further questions about using the service on copyright.com, please contact:

	Copyright Clearance Center	
Phone: +1-(978) 750-8400	Fax: +1-(978) 750-4470	E-mail: info@copyright.com

NOTICE TO THE READER

The Publisher has taken reasonable care in the preparation of this book but makes no expressed or implied warranty of any kind and assumes no responsibility for any errors or omissions. No liability is assumed for incidental or consequential damages in connection with or arising out of information contained in this book. The Publisher shall not be liable for any special, consequential, or exemplary damages resulting, in whole or in part, from the readers' use of, or reliance upon, this material. Any parts of this book based on government reports are so indicated and copyright is claimed for those parts to the extent applicable to compilations of such works.

Independent verification should be sought for any data, advice or recommendations contained in this book. In addition, no responsibility is assumed by the Publisher for any injury and/or damage to persons or property arising from any methods, products, instructions, ideas or otherwise contained in this publication.

This publication is designed to provide accurate and authoritative information with regards to the subject matter covered herein. It is sold with the clear understanding that the Publisher is not engaged in rendering legal or any other professional services. If legal or any other expert assistance is required, the services of a competent person should be sought. FROM A DECLARATION OF PARTICIPANTS JOINTLY ADOPTED BY A COMMITTEE OF THE AMERICAN BAR ASSOCIATION AND A COMMITTEE OF PUBLISHERS.

Library of Congress Cataloging-in-Publication Data

ISBN: 979-8-89113-303-7

Published by Nova Science Publishers, Inc. † New York

Contents

Preface vii

Acknowledgment xi

Chapter 1 **Accurate Word Alignment Induction for Bangla-Odia Using the EM Algorithm** 1
Bishwa Ranjan Das, Hima Bindu Maringanti and Niladri Sekhar Dash

Chapter 2 **An Automated Attendance System with Temperature and Face Mask Detection** 17
Ch. Kalyan Gopi, D. Sudha and K. Srujan Raju

Chapter 3 **Stock Market Analysis and Prediction Using Long Short Term Memory 6+** 31
Padmavathi Nayak, Hitaarth Jainn, Gouri Shetty Ramesh, Jammula Srini and Bandarwar Shruthika

Chapter 4 **Network Anomaly Detection Using a Random Forest Classifier** 51
T. Subburaj, K. Srujan Raju, N. M. Sinchana, K. Suthendran and Voruganti Naresh Kumar

Chapter 5 **A Comprehensible Decision Tree Based on LDA and PCA** 65
Asit Patra, Monalisa Jena and Satchidananda Dehuri

Chapter 6 **Image Steganography Using Deep Neural Networks** 91
Reddy Madhavi K., K. Pranitha, Nagendar Yamsani, Mohmad Ahmed Ali, K. Srujan Raju and Balijapalli Prathyusha

Chapter 7	Machine Learning on the Farm Animal Health Care System: A Review 101	
	Goddeti Mallikarjun and Dr.V. A. Narayana	
Chapter 8	Social Media Behavior Prediction Using Sentiment Analysis 113	
	Kurakula Arun Kumar, Sanjana Maankar, K. Sai Sahithi, P. Tharun Sai Reddy and K. Srujan Raju	
Chapter 9	Ultra-Wide Band Electromagnetic Band Gap (EBG) Antenna with WIMAX, WLAN and Satellite Downlink Communication Band Notching 129	
	Pakala Raveendra Babu and Rama Krishna Dasari	
Chapter 10	Hand Gesture Recognition Using a Deep Learning Model 147	
	J. Avanija, Thoutireddy Shilpa, Chikati Madhava Rao, Nagendar Yamsani and K. Srujan Raju	
Chapter 11	A Study on Blockchain-Cloud Hybrid Model-Based Healthcare Systems 161	
	Swatisipra Das and Minati Mishra	

About the Editors 175

Index 177

Preface

Information and knowledge management forms an integral part of the learning management system (LMS) that is relied on in the delivery of modern education and academic system. Dissemination of knowledge is effectively managed with the adoption of LMS. The pandemic period witnessed the accelerated and massive use of the LMS with the adoption of online classes, which, to a great extent mitigated the educational needs of society. In the present era of increased reliance on online methods of imparting education and the introduction of the digital university in the last year Union budget presentation, information, and knowledge management has assumed greater proportion and the world is now experiencing a greater reliance on it. From this perspective, the edited book can certainly contribute to knowledge building and management of delivery mechanisms.

We choose this title of the book because we are excited about the science of Information and knowledge management as an integrated science that focuses on the study and design of intelligent computational systems including knowledge of logic and basic probability, calculus, data structure, engineering optimization, and matrix theory to develop the concepts to solve a given problem

The Book is systematically organized into 11 chapters so that the reader can find information more easily on the coverage and structure of the Book. It covers topics of current interest to the researchers, academicians, industrial, and scientists, and prepares them to appreciate the field and prepares them for discussion on further technological concepts of Information and Knowledge Systems (IKS) it attempts to simplify the topic as much as possible so that the researchers can grasp the complex field of the IKS.

The various topics of the book have been explained in clear and simple language. Readers will be able to appreciate the concept of Information and Knowledge Systems together with their engineering applications. In various fields of real-life, recent trends and fashions to carry out day-to-day tasks are expanding rapidly. The book deals with the latest developments in the field of Information and Knowledge System technology and the building blocks.

Chapter 1 contributed by Das, et al. on "Accurate Word Alignment Induction for Bangla-Odia Using EM Algorithm" analysed about the theme Natural Language Processing (NLP) and have discussed that NLP is a branch of artificial intelligence within computer science. They focused on helping computers to understand the way that humans write and speak, provides the tools to enhance data and analysed both linguistic and statistical data, It uses the Expectation-Maximization (EM) method to demonstrate extremely accurate word alignment between Bangla and Odia. The biggest obstacle and most difficult task in word alignment is finding a solution to the "word divergence" or "lexical divergence" problem. According to them, "The only way to solve it, even though the EM algorithm cannot, is to use a bilingual dictionary, commonly referred to as a lexical database, which is based on scientific study and tested mathematically".

Chapter 2 contributed by Gopi, et al., on "Automated Attendance System with Temperature and Face Mask Detection" threw light on using biometric systems that may cause a problem of spreading the virus as it needs physical contact to provide entry & attendance to an individual. The Implementation is done using Raspberry Pi and Python script to train the model on a variety of possibilities and has a large, varied dataset so the model can identify and detect face masks and temperature in real-time.

In Chapter 3, Nayak, et al. have discussed on "Stock Market Analysis and Prediction using Long Short-Term Memory" and presented that the analysis of the stock market helps in clever and thoughtful investment and hence brings heavy returns on investment. To predict the patterns of the stock price the historical data, statistical models, and Support Vector Machine (SVM) adds a benchmark check to the estimation and in deciding investments.

In Chapter 4, Raju, et al., have made a thorough discussion on "Network Anomaly Detection using Random Forest Classifier", and draws that Network-attacks are looking to be a more complex framework. Signature-based Intrusion Detection Systems (SIDS) and Anomaly-based Intrusion Detection Systems (AIDS) are the two types of Intrusion Detection Systems (IDS) in automatic intrusion detection.

In Chapter 5, Patra, et al., have presented a novel work on "A Comprehensible Decision Tree Based on LDA and PCA". They make a comparative analysis between the performance of a decision tree known as the Classification and Regression Tree (CART), and the decision tree (CART) based on PCA (PCA-DT) and LDA (LDA-DT) by considering a few real-life datasets.

Madhavi, et al., in Chapter 6 discussed on "Image Steganography Using Deep Neural Network" and write that they endeavour to put a regular variety of images inside one more picture of the same size. In conclusion, they view numerous famous steganographic strategies that encode secret messages inside the "least significant bits" of "carrier image", their methodology packs and conveys the secret image's portrayal across accessible pieces as a whole.

Chapter 7 written by the authors Mallikarjun, et al., focussed on "Machine Learning on Farm Animal Health Care System: A Review" write that machine learning is an essential study subject because it discovers patterns in massive amounts of data. The use of latest the technologies like machine learning will help the farmer to predict the farm animal's disease with good accuracy. In conclusion, they classify and contrast two types of machine learning: unsupervised and supervised.

Chapter 8 authored by Kumar, et al., enlightens reader on "Social Media Behavior Prediction Using Sentiment Analysis" write that utilizing social media posts, comments, likes, and offers, it is possible to anticipate customer behaviour. Posts and comments of customers can be monitored while they are being broken down.

Chapter 9 discussed by researchers Raveendrababu and Ramakrishna in their article on "Ultra-Wide Band Electromagnetic Band Gap (EBG) Antenna with WIMAX, WLAN & Satellite downlink communication Band Notching" write that Electromagnetic Band Gaps (EBGs) structures with fractal and two via edge-located (TVEL) characteristics were created by etching an open loop slot into the radiating patch, which was then connected to a faulty microstrip structure (DMS) frequency bands now come in three levels. They investigated the impedance and radiation properties of the UWB antenna, teste,d the simulated, and measured data.

Chapter 10 authored by Avanija, et al. discussed on "Hand Gesture Recognition Using Machine Learning and DeepLearning" focussed that convolutional neural networks are a type of artificial neural network inspired by the visual cortex. Image Data Generator applies a series of random translations, rotations, and so on to each image in the batch. The CNN algorithm is used in the proposed system to extract image features.

Chapter 11 described by the authors Das and Mishra in their paper "A Study on Blockchain-Cloud hybrid model-based Healthcare Systems" have analysed the block-chain cloud hybrid model in healthcare systems. The Block Chain-Cloud combined model-based healthcare systems eliminate third-party dependency, reduce the implementation cost and provide better scalability to handle the continuously growing health records.

In this book, the reader will be able to:

i) Have a solid foundation in Information and Knowledge Systems (IKS).
ii) Explore the different techniques of knowledge representations and constraint satisfaction problems.
iii) Understand the different principles to solve problems of learning management systems (LMS) by various algorithms.

Manaswini Pradhan
Satchidananda Dehuri
Editors

Acknowledgment

We wish to thank the researchers and practitioners in the fields of Information Systems, Artificial Intelligence, Knowledge Management and Decision Support for extended and immense support all through the preparation of this edited book.

We express our deep sense of gratitude to Professor Santosh Kumar Tripathy, Hon'ble Vice-Chancellor, of our university for his interest in research activities and encouragement for research endeavours. His constant encouragement was a source of inspiration for all faculties.

We acknowledge our obligation to our teachers, friends, and fellow members of the teaching staff at the Fakir Mohan University, Balasore for kind cooperation for fulfillment of the edited book.

We owe a lot to our chapter authors for their contributions and relentless service and continued help in collecting data and analyzing it for their research outcomes, and at various stages of the research study to complete their chapters.

We express our deep sense of gratitude and heartfelt thanks to our PhD and M.Phil. research scholars for their constant support in every work we undertook.

We express our gratefulness to the moderators, subject experts and Nova Science Publishers, Inc. for giving us an opportunity to undertake this book project to promote discussions on various organizational, technological, and socio-cultural aspects of research in the design and use of information and knowledge systems in organizations.

Manaswini Pradhan
Satchidananda Dehuri
Editors

Chapter 1

Accurate Word Alignment Induction for Bangla-Odia Using the EM Algorithm

Bishwa Ranjan Das[1,*]
Hima Bindu Maringanti[1]
and Niladri Sekhar Dash[2]

[1]Department of Computer Application, Maharaja Sriram Chandra Bhanjadeo University, Baripada, India
[2]Linguistic Research Unit, Indian Statistical Institute, Kolkata, India

Abstract

This study uses the Expectation-Maximization (EM) method to demonstrate extremely accurate word alignment between Bangla and Odia. The full mathematical process is built out and illustrated in this case using a series of examples from selected Bangla-Odia words. This EM approach works in conjunction with the "argmax function," which monitors the mapping between two or more words of the source and destination languages in sentences, to ascertain the highest probable probability value. It is possible to calculate the lexical link between the words in two parallel sentences, and the results show which word in the target language is aligned with which word in the source language. Iteratively computing some probability values in terms of maximum likelihood estimation (MLE) or looping the EM algorithm can be used to find the MLE or maximum a posterior (MAP) of parameters in the probabilities model, where the model depends on the latent variable that is not observed. The necessity for numerous machine learning techniques and mathematical modelling makes lexical alignment for translation one

---

[*] Corresponding Author's Email: biswadas.bulu@gmail.com.

In: Information and Knowledge Systems
Editors: Manaswini Pradhan and Satchidananda Dehurl
ISBN: 979-8-89113-303-7
© 2024 Nova Science Publishers, Inc.

of the hardest challenges to solve. We have made an effort to clarify the several lexical issues that come up when assessing bilingual literature that was translated from Bangla (the source language) to Odia in light of all of these challenges (as the target language). The biggest obstacle and most difficult task in word alignment is finding a solution to the "word divergence" or "lexical divergence" problem. The only way to solve it, despite the fact that the EM algorithm cannot, is to use a bilingual dictionary, commonly referred to as a lexical database, which is based on scientific study and tested totally mathematically. Bilingual dictionaries or lexical databases are widely used to address word divergence or lexical divergence issues at the phrase level. Finding single word units from the source text that are changed into multiword units in the target text presents the most problem.

Keywords: Odia, Bangla, probability, maximization, expectation, alignment, divergence

Introduction

Word alignment is a technique for identifying the exact and comparable term between two parallel corpora. This illustrates one of the word translation interactions between two or more parallel sentences. Word divergence is the process through which a term is occasionally translated by one or more words. The main goal of word alignment, assuming parallel sentences are provided, is to determine the correspondence between words in source and target sentences that may be one-to-one, one-to-many, or many-to-many. The solution offered by phrase-based translation is to pair up phrases or word groups in the target language with equivalent phrases in the source language. The terms in the source phrase are just assigned the number 0 if the target language does not have a suitable translation for them.

Related Work

Various using hybrid methods to perform local word grouping in Hindi and other methods such as dictionary search, transliteration similarity, and expected English words, closest aligned neighbors, etc. Word alignment details using different usages. Let's take a closer look at the probability values between small and large pairs of statements (Aswani et al., 2005). This section briefly describes various topics, issues, and challenges. It also details the different types of approaches (Das et al., 2020). Using expected value maximization algorithms and statistical techniques, the majority of problems are explored and resolved with great care, and the overall notion is presented clearly and precisely. Here, most problems and problems are solved (Das et al., 2020). The one-to-one and many-to-one mapping approaches for the Bengali-Odia vocabulary divergence issue are discussed in this article. To map parallel Hindi and English terms in sentences, use a word dictionary (Dubey et al., 2012). Using a variety of techniques, including the border detection approach, the minimal distance function, dictionary searches, and so on, we carried out automatic word alignment (Jindal et al., 2011). The most crucial aspect of machine translation is compound word spitting, which divides a word into its various meanings. It explores the difficulties of translating from one language to another and methodically addresses the various ways, their advantages and disadvantages (Kohen n Knight 2003). An innovative stochastic model of word placement is presented in this paper. In this approach, word placement corresponds to many sorts of linguistically driven placement. A new semi-supervised learning technique is implemented for a new job that involves concurrently predicting word alignment and alignment type (Mansouri et al., 2017). Defines the alignment between pairs of such statements. A set of five statistical models of the translation process are explained, algorithms are given to estimate the parameters of these models, and a set of sentence pairs that are translations of one another are shown (Peter F. Brown et al., 1993). This book offers a thorough and understandable introduction to the main methods applied in statistical machine translation. You can easily convert from source to target using a variety of online MT tools. B. Babelfish, Bing Translator, and Google Translator via Yahoo and AltaVista (Philipp Koehn 2010).

Expectation- Maximization (EM) Algorithm

The EM approach is used to iteratively find the maximum likelihood (MLE) or maximum a posteriori (MAP) estimates of the model's parameters when a statistical model is an unobserved latent variable. The EM iteration is an expected value step (E) that maximizes the computation of the parameter that maximizes the expected logarithm and provides a function of the expected value of the log-likelihood that is evaluated using the current estimate of the parameter. Steps that alternate (M). At level E, it might be found. This algorithm's primary objective is to identify the best outcome or value.

Problems Faced

Different types of problem are faced during word alignments.t. One-to-many, many-to-one, many-to-many, named entity problem, one having multiple alignment. But how to solve these by ML or DL?

Word Alignment with Methodology

This study suggests that, given the Odia set O represented by $P(B \mid O)$, a conditional probability model of the Bangla set B be trained. A model is said to contain an index, which is a collection of parameters, if it has a set of n pairings of datasets D that are understood to be transformations of one another. $(B_1, O_1), (B_2, O_2), (B_3, O_3),..., (B_n, O_n)$ are all identical to D. In this scenario, each index n represents a distinct pair. There are several ways to define $P(B|O)$. The Odia clause O is represented by an array of index words J $(O_1, O_2, O_3,..., O_J)$, and an array of I words serve as the representation for the Bangla clause B. Here, it is reasonable to assume that every Bengali language is a perfect match for one or more Odia languages. This may be expressed as an array "a" of length I. Its members are [$a_1, a_2, a_3,... a_i$], with $a_1, a_2, a_3,...,$ and a_i serving as the one-to-one placement variables. The alignment variable a_i is acceptable in the [0, J] range of values. The Bengali index and Odia Oi were in alignment. None of the Odia words are aligned with Bi if a_i is zero. It's referred to as null alignment. Look at two sentences in Odia and Bengali.

Bangla Sentence

নিজেদের দাবি নিয়ে নির্মাণকার্য বন্ধ করার জন্য কৃষকদের সংগঠনের মধ্যে আলোড়ন সৃষ্টি হয়েছে।

Transliteration

"Nijeder dAbiniye nirmAn kAryya bandha karArjanna krishakder sangaThener madhye aloRon srisTi hayechhe".

Odia Sentence

ନିଜର ଅଧିକାରକୁ ନେଇ ନିର୍ମାଣ କାର୍ଯ୍ୟ ବନ୍ଦକରିବାକୁ କୃଷକସଂଗଠନ ଗୁଡ଼ିକରେ ହତଚମଟ ସୃଷ୍ଟି ହୋଇଯାଇଛି ।

Transliteration

"Nijara adhikaraku nei nirmana karjya bandakaribaku krushakasangathana gudikare hatachamata shrusti haijachhi".

According to the length, an Odia sentence has a word count of 12, whereas Bengali sentences have a total word count of 14. Where I and J stand for the respective Bengali and Odia sentence lengths. The word indexes are B1, B2, B3, BI and O1, O2, O3,..., OJ for both sentences. The value of the alignment array "a" is "1,2,3,4,5,6,7,7,8,9,9,10,11,12". The probabilistic model proposes a simple procedure to generate a Bangla Odia set. The first step is to choose the length I in accordance with the distribution P (I|J), in this case P (14|12). The placement of each Odia word in the standard corpus (ai=j|J; ILCI-Indian Language Corpora Initiative, Government of India) is then done in accordance with where it should be in the corresponding Bangla sentence (or null). The final stage in the transformation of each Bengali Bi is the alignment of the Odia P(Bi|O) probability distribution function. As a result, P (Nijara|Nijeder), P (adhikaraku|dabi), P (nei|nie), and so forth are all increased in this alignment. The likelihood of the Bangla set and its Odia conditional alignment is the total of these probabilities.

$$P(B, a|O) = P(I|J) \prod_{i=1}^{I} P(a_i|J) \cdot P(B_i|O_{a_i}) \tag{1}$$

Simply put, there are two tables of numbers: P(I|J) for all pairs of sentence lengths I and J and P(B|O) for all contiguous Bangla and Odia word pairs. The set of valid assignments to these tables must abide by the basic principles of probability because these numbers relate to probabilities.

$$\forall_{O,B} P(B|O) \in [0,1] \tag{2}$$

$$\forall_O \sum_B P(B|O) = 1 \tag{3}$$

Maximum Likelihood Estimation

Pay attention to P (B | O) and use maximum likelihood estimation to estimate the approximation to observe the alignment (MLE). Talk about good sentence structure before beginning the word placement between Bengali and Odia. The condition depicted in the English to French translation, however, does not exist in Bengali-Odia [19]. For instance, Bengali-Odia does not have the word pairings that most French words do with English. Here, we introduce the MLE function from the standpoint of comprehension in order to calculate the likelihood of the supplied parameters.

$$\prod_{n=1}^{N} P_\theta(B^{(n)}, a^{(n)} | O^{(n)}) = \prod_{n=1}^{N} P(I^{(n)} | J^{(n)}) \prod_{i=1}^{I^{(n)}} P(a_i^{(n)} | J^{(n)}) \cdot P(B_i^{(n)} | O_{a_i}^{(n)})$$

(4)

N represents the quantity of sentences. Every sentence's index number is "n," its alignment is "a," every sentence in Bangla is "I" long, and every phrase in Odia is "J" long. The time has come to employ a probability function to ascertain the highest value because our data (and value) are very likely to match this model now that the parameters have been calculated and collected.

$$\hat{\theta} = \frac{argmax}{\theta} \prod_{i=1}^{N} P_\theta(B^{(n)}, a^{(n)} | O^{(n)})$$

(5)

In equation (5), For each and every word in a sentence, where $\hat{\theta}$ uses the argmax function to find the word alignment with the highest probability value. When it comes to machine translation, the issue is fundamentally one of looking through an infinite pool of potential texts. After translation in accordance with the corpus, just one sentence is chosen from a variety of potential sentences. When the data provided by our model is completely observed, there is a closed-form solution for $\hat{\theta}$, but the search problem in this case is straightforward. The procedure or model that is described here was really started by an algorithm created to learn from our fictitiously aligned data. It is really straightforward: after scanning and analyzing the data, the alignments of each pair of Bangla-Odia words are added up. All counts (means probability values) are normalized by the frequency of the relevant Bangla word appearing in any alignment to determine the probabilities (aligned word pair Bangla-Odia). This results in the relatively straightforward technique that is discussed here. Although there is a closed-form solution for $\hat{\theta}$ when the data given by our model is fully observed, the search issue in this instance is simple. An algorithm designed to learn from our fictitiously aligned data actually launched the process or model that is explained here. It is quite simple: each pair of Bangla-Odia words' alignments are totaled up after the data has been scanned and examined. To calculate the probabilities, all counts (means probability values) are normalized by the frequency with which the relevant Bangla word appears in any alignment (aligned word pair Bangla-Odia). This leads to the comparatively simple technique that is described here.

Algorithm 1

St 1. Initialize all counts to 0
St 2. For each n value between 1 to N
St 3. For each i value between 1 to I
St 4. For each j value between 1 to J
St 5. Compare ai = j upto ni.e. i value
St 6. Count [(Bi, Oj)] ++
St 7. Count [Oj]++
St 8. For each (Bi, Oj) value in count do
St 9. P(B|O) = Count(B,O)/Count(O)

To calculate the count, algorithm 1 runs through each pair of words. This sentence length estimation uses a quadratic formula. It may be sufficient to simply loop through the alignment variables to collect the linear counts if this is not strictly necessary. However, when dealing with instances of unobserved alignments that have shown to be extensions of this approach, it is helpful to conceive of it as looking at all word pairs. Here, after a number of iterations, the alignment probability is determined using two equations. Although this algorithm is not completely speculative, it does need a small sample of observed alignment sentences gathered from bilingual annotations. Although this small sample of observational data has undergone training, the result is a poor estimate of. As a result, the accurate estimation of is applied using the EM algorithm. The primary issue with MLE is that the alignment 'a' is frequently ignored. Because of this, using the EM algorithm to learn the parameters of a latent variable model like IBM Model 1 is the most effective method. EM offers two benefits: it replaces the number of alignment connections that were observed with the predicted number of alignment links that were computed using the previously estimated. The previous estimate is then used to compare the projected count to and is subsequently improved upon. The number observed and the number of anticipated alignment links are both required. Other advantages or sources of inspiration exist for the MLE EM method. Equation (4) must therefore be significantly altered in order to account for the new reality.

$$\prod_{n=1}^{N} P_\theta(B^{(n)}|O^{(n)}) = \prod_{n=1}^{N} P(I^{(n)}|J^{(n)}) \sum_{a^{(n)}} \prod_{i=1}^{I^{(n)}} P(a_i^{(n)}|J^{(n)}) \cdot P(B_i^{(n)}|O_{a_i}^{(n)})$$

(6)

Here, the likelihood of the observed data is still maximized, but the third term is deleted and should not be taken into account in the fourth term because the observed data does not include alignment. In other words, since the alignments are not visible, a precise alignment or output is obtained by combining the probabilities for every alignment that the data might have produced. This is due to the probability rule's assertion that it provides B's marginal probabilities. The set that needs to be maximized is this one. The entire alignment conflicts with the analytical solution, which is a minor fault. However, an algorithm can be used to resolve any issue. However, this technique highlights issues or inaccuracies such as the anticipated number of linkages that may be estimated using Bayes' theorem, much like MLE does.

$$P(a_i = j \mid B, O) = \frac{P(B|a_i = j, O)P(a_i = j|O)}{P(B|O)} = \frac{P(B, a_i = j|O)}{P(B|O)}$$

(7)

Here, posterior probabilities calculate the proportion of connections between Bi and Oj that are aligned. The significance of likelihood after many people are aware of the linkage rate. According to Equation 7, posterior probabilities are calculated by dividing the total probability of all alignments, including the one that connects Bi and Oj, by the total probability of all possible alignments. The resultant value is a probability number as a result. The link value is raised by 1 for MLE. Specifically, a count variable if you notice a connection between two words and a count variable of 0 otherwise.

As a result, the later probability value falls between 0 and 1. It conveys our skepticism regarding Bi and Oj possible romantic connection. In all likelihood, you are not connected if the value is close to 0. Your connection is almost probably established if the value is close to 1. If it's in the middle, I have no idea (i.e., there is absolutely no relationship). The likelihood after a possible event should be used instead of the quantity of observed occurrences, according to EM's first key principle. In other words, we must determine the probabilities that follow them. It was observed.

$$\frac{P(B, a_i=j|O)}{P(B|O)} = \frac{P(I|J)\Sigma_{a:a_i=j}\prod_{i\prime}^{I} P(a_i|J).P(B_{i\prime}|O_{a_i\prime})}{P(I|J)\Sigma_a \prod_{i=1}^{I} P(a_i|J) P(B_i|O_{a_i})} = \frac{\Sigma_{a:a_i=j}\prod_{i\prime=0}^{I} P(B_{i\prime}|O_{a_{i\prime}})}{\Sigma_a \prod_{i=1}^{I} P(B_i|O_{a_i})} \quad (8)$$

Now the sentence length P(I|J) is able to cancel, because P(ai|J) is uniform, the expression $\prod_{i=0}^{I} P(a_i|J)$ is constant across all alignment of the sentence. Now it is also cancelled out. This expression is written purely in terms of lexical translation probability. Both the numerator and denominator in equation (8) are sum over exponentially many terms. Let's rewrite the equation (8) slightly by enumerating the summation over each element of a.

$$\frac{\Sigma_{a:a_i=j}\prod_{i\prime=0}^{I} P(B_{i\prime}|O_{a_{i\prime}})}{\Sigma_a \prod_{i=1}^{I} P(B_i|O_{a_i})} = \frac{P(B_i|O_j)\Sigma_{a_1=0}^{J}\cdots\Sigma_{a_{i-1}=0}^{J}\Sigma_{a_I=0}^{J}\prod_{i\prime=0}^{I} P(B_{i\prime}|O_{a_{i\prime}})}{\Sigma_{a_1=0}^{J}\cdots\Sigma_{a_I=0}^{J}\prod_{i=1}^{I} P(B_i|O_{a_i})} \quad (9)$$

By making use of the denominator's regularity, a sum over product of precisely I term, the equation is made easier. To finish the summing over values of ai, P(B1|O1) must first be multiplied by all permutations of the probabilities of word translations from B2 through BI. Adding up all of the values in a1 (means 1st alignment). All combinations of the probability of translations of the terms B2 through B1 are multiplied by P(Bi|Oj). Using distributivity to your advantage, go on to the sum over values of a1 inside the product over values of i. Repeat this process for the sum over values of a2, a3, and so forth. Simply change the numerator's sums and products, and simply remove the majority of the terms.

$$\frac{P(B_i|O_j)\prod_{i\prime=0}^{I}\Sigma_{a_1=0}^{J}\cdots\Sigma_{a_{i-1}=0}^{J}\Sigma_{a_{i+1}=0}^{J}\cdots\Sigma_{a_I=0}^{J} P(B_{i\prime}|O_{a_{i\prime}})}{\prod_{i=1}^{I}\Sigma_{a_1=0}^{J}\cdots\Sigma_{a_I=0}^{J} P(B_i|O_{a_i})} = \frac{P(B_i|O_j)}{\Sigma_{a_i=1}^{J} P(B_i|O_{a_i})} \quad (10)$$

The calculation of posterior probabilities P (ai = j | B, O) for the linear number of parameter P (B | O) is shown in equation (10). The anticipated decimal number of links can be calculated. Counts are separated like MLE and cumulative across the entire dataset. This indicates that MLE is split by the anticipated number of linkages. The expected step (E step) in EM is used to calculate the expected count, while the M step is used to normalize the data (maximized). There is a small problem with this placement. This implies that the first item to check for should be the parameters used to determine the expected value. This problem is not lethal, though. Assign to the initial value represented by 0, then compute the expected count for 0 to obtain the MLE, and then compute the expected count for 1 to obtain the MLE. The predicted count is then determined using 1. Therefore, use estimate 2. The second key principle guiding the EM algorithm is the notion of comparatively improving the estimate. To do this, EM has been added to Algorithm 1.

Algorithm 2

    Step1 k=0
    Step2 Initialize θ_0
    Step3 repeat
    Step4 k=k+1
    Step5 Initialize all counts to 0
    Step6 for each n in [1, 2, 3,......N] do
    Step7 for each i in [1, 2, 3...,I(n)] do
    Step8 z=0
    Step9 for each j in [1,2,3,....J(n)] do
    Step10 $z +\!= P_{\theta_{k-1}}(B_i^{(n)}|O_j^{(n)})$
    Step11 for each j in [1, 2, 3...J(n)] do
    Step12 $c = P_{\theta_{k-1}}(B_i^{(n)}|O_j^{(n)})/z$
    Step13 $count\left[<B_i^{(n)}, O_j^{(n)}>\right] +\!= c$
    Step14 $count\left[e_j\right] +\!= c$
    Step15   for each <B,O> in count do
    Step16 $P_{\theta_k}(B|O) = count(B,O)/count(O)$

There are two θ_0 responses. Here are two important aspects of EM. The first is that the likelihood of θ_i will always be greater than that of θ_{i-1}). The second factor is that Model 1's likelihood function is convex. These characteristics imply that the highest probability estimate for EM on IBM model 1 will eventually be accurate. Recursively or repeatedly determining the value of 0 (a long time). The empirical response is considerably different. The majority of people only run three to five EM iterations, and [Moore 2004] demonstrates that in this situation, heuristic initialization of _0 can greatly increase accuracy. The core idea is that the E-step creates a function that lowers the true (log) likelihood and touches this likelihood at the current parameter setting, and the M-step chooses new parameters to maximize this lower limit. When EM is run, good value of θ is searched and that θ is used for predicting the 'a'. This 'a' is assigned to the highest probability value and indicates as $\hat{a}$.

$$\hat{a} = \underset{a}{argmax}\, P(a|O,B) \tag{11}$$

This is very easy, the alignment factor over the Bangla words.

$$\hat{a}_i = \underset{a_i}{argmax}\, P(I|J) \prod_{i=1}^{I} P(a_i|J).P(B_i|O_{a_i}) \tag{12}$$

Since the only quantity that depends on a_i is $P(B_i|O_{a_i})$, this reduces to

$$\hat{a}_i = \underset{a_i}{argmax}\, P(B_i|O_{a_i}) \tag{13}$$

Algorithm 3

This happens in algorithm 3 is most Probable Alignment
Step1 for each n in [1,2,3, ...N] do
Step2 for each i in [1,2,3,....I(n)] do
Step3 best_probability = 0
Step4 best_j = 0
Step5 for each j in [1,2,3,.....J(n)] do
Step6 if $P\left(f_i^{(n)}\middle|e_j^n\right) > best_{prob}$ then
Step7 $best\_probability = P(f_i^{(n)}|e_j^{(n)})$

Step8 $best\_j = j$
Step9 align(n, i, best_j)

$$C(B_i \leftrightarrow O_j; B^s \leftrightarrow O^s) = \frac{P(O_j|B_i)}{\sum_x P(x|B_i)} * (\#B_i \in B^s) * (\#O_j \in O^s) E - step \qquad (14)$$

Here C = expected count of $B_i \leftrightarrow O_j$ mapping in the context of the parallel corpus $B^s \leftrightarrow O^s$. $\#B_i \in B^s$ = no. of time B_i appears in B^s. $\#O_j \in O^s$ = no. of time O_j appears in O^s. 's' refers to a parallel sentence pair.

$$P(O_j|B_i) = \frac{\sum_s C(B_i \leftrightarrow O_j; B^s \leftrightarrow O^s)}{\sum_s \sum_x C(B_i \leftrightarrow x; B^s \leftrightarrow O^s)} M - step \qquad (15)$$

The ratio of the counts of P(Bi|Oj) mapping to the count of mapping of, $B_i \leftrightarrow x$ where x is any word in all the parallel sentences, is used to determine P(Oj|Bi). It has been demonstrated that the likelihood of the data in this situation, parallel corpora, increases monotonically with each repetition of the E-step and M-step. Entropy can be thought of as progressing in the direction of lessening. Therefore, the iterative procedure is greedy. The data probability expression might have become trapped in a local minimum if it weren't convex and guaranteed a global minimum.

An Odia translation of the Bangla text B=b1, b2, b3, bj is O=o1, o2, o3... oi. One seeks out the Odia sentence with the highest probability P(O|B). It can be expressed as

P(O|B)=P(O)P(B|O)/P(B) (16)

Finding the translation that is most likely to occur will result in the noisy channel model for statistical machine translation because the denominator is independent of O.

e*= argmax P(O|B) (17)

=argmaxP(O)(P(B|O) (18)

where P(O) denotes the language model and P(B|O) denotes the translation model. Phrase-based translation is frequently the only choice for many-to-one and one-to-many global alignment when word divergence is present. A corpus focused on the agriculture domain has been used to map the terms using a bilingual Bangla-Odia lexicon. Comparing the words one to one reveal that they translate rather well.

Results and Discussion

A modest number of phrases (about 5,000 words) and over 50,000 words are stored in agricultural-based multilingual dictionaries for simple access by monitoring their arrangement. As shown in equation, all observed directions are trained to provide a fair estimate of (5). Get a good quote by treating it more like a date. One-to-one, many-to-one, and many-to-one word correspondences are all included in this. The first possibility is connections (as a one-to-one mapping). By calculating the probability values, the model learns to connect the most comparable words from two parallel phrases after one iteration. A second repetition demonstrates that the probability value of the present word is less likely than the relationship between earlier identical words. The ideal technique to determine sentence probability and word-to-word placement is therefore to use bigrams and trigrams. Every probability value is determined using a bigram with a table or matrix structure. Between the words in each parallel phrase, the expected number, modified expected number, and modified alignment probability value are calculated. The updated alignment probability gives words in parallel sentences a more accurate approximation. An improvement in probability distribution can already be seen in the average entropy value for an EM alignment of 1.4, which is lower than the average entropy value for a heuristic alignment of 1.53 and 1.4. Other mathematical procedures can be used to increase this percentage even higher.

Figure 1 indicates how the accuracy level increases monotonically. The x-axis represents probability and y-axis represents the number of sentences.

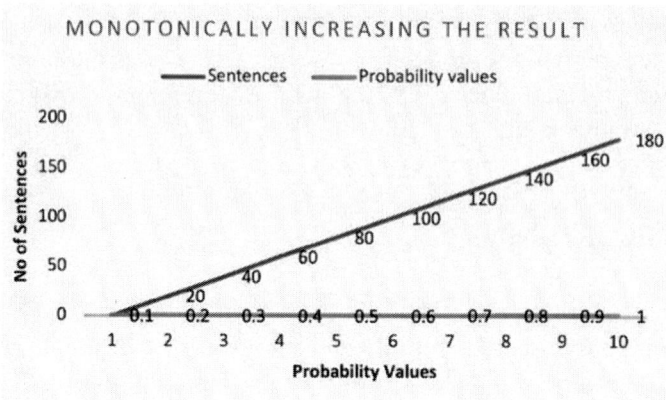

Figure 1. Monotonically Increasing the Result.

Conclusion

First of all, assuming the bilingual corpus is properly positioned at the sentence level, it is simple to achieve machine-by-word translation when translating from one language to another. Most often, sentence-based translations and bilingual dictionaries can resolve issues like one-to-many and many-to-one placements. The bilingual dictionary serves as a Bengali-Odia correspondent between the two languages on a one-to-one, one-to-many, and many-to-one basis. When there are word differences, expression-level translations might be a preferable alternative. The most appropriate word pair (Bengali-Odia) between the two languages is found using the expected value maximization algorithm, from which the highest probability value is achieved. In order to help you locate a word's precise location in your target language, it also translates words by word and sentences by sentences. When there is a large amount of machine translation data, one of the primary factors is time complexity. As a result, you must exercise caution if you want better outcomes. This optimization task is difficult. You don't need to make your space less difficult because the corpus data is enormous. You need to add more space because memory is a problem. Otherwise, NLP- or data-based study treatises will be skimmed through.

References

Aswani. Niraj, and Robert Gaizauskas, "Aligning words in English-Hindi parallel corpora," *Association for Computational Linguistics*, Vol.19, Pp. 115-118, 2005.

Bishwa Ranjan Das, Hima Bindu Maringanti, Niladri Sekhar Dash, "Word Alignment in bilingual text for Bangla to Odia Machine Translation", Presented in *the International Conference on Languaging and Translating: Within and Beyond* on 21-23, Feb 2020, IIT Patna, India.

Bishwa Ranjan Das, Hima Bindu Maringanti, Niladri Sekhar Dash, "Challenges Faced in Machine Learning-Based Bangla-Odia Word Alignment for Machine Translation", Presented in *the 42nd International Conference of Linguistic Society of India* (ICOLSI-42) on 10-12 Dec 2020, GLA University, Mathura, UP, India.

Bishwa Ranjan Das, Hima Bindu Maringanti, Niladri Sekhar Dash, "Bangla-Odia Word Alignment using EM algorithm for Machine Translation", published in the *journal of Maharaja Sriram Chandra Bhanjadeo* (erstwhile North Orissa) University, Baripada, India.

Dubey, Shweta, and Tarun Dhar Diwan, "Supporting Large English-Hindi Parallel Corpus using Word Alignment", *International Journal of Computer Applications*, Vol 49, Pp 16-19, 2012.

Jindal, Karuna, Vishal Goyal & Shikha Jindal, "Automatic word Aligning algorithm for Hindi-Punjabi Parallel Text", *International Conference on Information Systems for Indian languages*, pp 180-184, 2011.

Koehn. Philipp, and Kevin Knight, "Empirical Methods for Compounding Splitting", EACL '03 *Association for Computational Linguistics* - Volume 1, Pages 187-193, April 12 - 17, 2003.

Mansouri, Anahita Bigvand, Te Bu, and Anoop Sarkar, "Joint Prediction of Word Alignment with Alignment Types", *Transactions of the Association for Computational Linguistics*, Vol. 5, Pp. 501-514, 2017.

Peter F. Brown, Stephen A. Della Pietra, Vincent J. Della Pietra, and Robert L. Mercer. "The mathematics of statistical machine translation: Parameter estimation," *Computational Linguistics*, Vol 19(2): Pp 263-311, June 1993.

Philipp Koehn. Statistical Machine Translation. 2010.

Robert C. Moore, Improving IBM word-alignment model 1. In Proceedings of the Association for Computational Linguistics, 2004.

Songyot. Theerawat, and Songyot, David Chiang, "Improving Word Alignment using Word Similarity", *Empirical methods in Natural Language Processing*, pp. 1840-1845, 2014.

Tidemann, Jorg., "Word alignment step by step". In Proceedings of *the 12th Nordic Conference on Computational Linguistics*, pages 216-227, 1999, University of Trondheim, Norway.

Tidemann, Jorg.,"Combining clues for word alignment", In *Proceedings of the 10th Conference of the European Chapter of the Association for Computational Linguistics* (EACL), pages 339-346, Budapest, Hungary, April 2003.

Tidemann, Jorg. "Word to word alignment strategies", *International Conference on Computational Linguistics*, 2004.

Bhattacharyya, Pushpak. *"Machine Translation,"* CRC Press, 2017 Print.
Daniel Jurafsky & James H. Martin, "Speech and Language Processing", 4th Edition, Pearson, 2011.
https://en.wikipedia.org/wiki/Expectation%E2%80%93maximization_algorithm.
https://www.cs.sfu.ca/~anoop/students/anahita_mansouri/anahita-depth-report.pdf.
http://citeseerx.ist.psu.edu/viewdoc/download?doi=10.1.1.421.5497&rep=rep1&type=pdf

Chapter 2

An Automated Attendance System with Temperature and Face Mask Detection

Ch. Kalyan Gopi[1]
D. Sudha[1]
and K. Srujan Raju[2]
[1]Department of ECE, CMR College of Engineering and Technology,
Hyderabad, Telangana, India
[2]Department of CSE, CMR Technical Campus,
Hyderabad, Telangana, India

Abstract

Amid the pandemic, people have realized the importance of face masks and the effects of not wearing one, now more than ever. As all the organizations are calling their employees back to the office there is no safety system to monitor and make sure all the employees are following the safety guidelines. This proposed system introduces a face mask detection model along with a temperature check so that basic safety precautions are maintained. Face mask detection and recognition is an upgrade to the existing biometric systems. Using biometric systems may cause a problem of spreading the virus as it needs physical contact to provide entry & attendance to an individual. This system also includes a contactless entry system which can be used by any organization. This system can also scan and detect the temperature of a person and detect whether the person is wearing a mask or not. If the mask is detected and the temperature is normal, he/she can scan their ID card and enter the office without any physical contact. The implementation is done using Raspberry Pi and Python script to train the model on a variety of possibilities and has a large, varied dataset so the model can identify and detect face masks and temperature in real-time.

In: Information and Knowledge Systems
Editors: Manaswini Pradhan and Satchidananda Dehurl
ISBN: 979-8-89113-303-7
© 2024 Nova Science Publishers, Inc.

Keywords: face mask, safety, temperature

Introduction

In recent years the world has seen advanced development in Science & Technology. It is possible for humans to achieve things that seemed impossible decades ago. Machine learning & Artificial Intelligence have helped a lot in easing our lives by achieving nearly impossible things.

In 2020, the world witnessed a deadly pandemic that took many lives, and many people suffered. The precautionary steps suggested by World Health Organization (WHO) to avoid this virus are by using face masks, maintaining social distancing, cleaning hands, and not touching eyes, nose and mouth.

The first wave of Covid-19 has left the world in a situation where there are a lot of restrictions and each individual should prioritize safety measures. In 2021 after the second wave of Covid-19, a new virus is found in people which is named Omicron. The symptoms are not fatal as Covid-19 but still, preventive measures need to be followed by everyone to avoid getting distorted by the virus.

As lockdown is not a permanent solution for this pandemic, all Businesses, Markets, Schools, Colleges, Transportation and Organizations need to run without any interruption as they are very crucial points in everyone's lives. As much as people are following all the safety norms, it is very important to closely watch the public at all times.

One crucial factor is using face masks at all times. Studies have proven that by wearing face masks people can reduce the chance of infection by the virus. By using face masks 80-85% of the risk can be avoided. AI and Deep learning can help to enforce the mask policy on each individual.

This project aims at designing a system to make sure that all the safety precautions are followed by each individual at an organization. This system provides attendance to an individual only if he/she is following the safety protocols. This system is equipped with a contactless temperature sensor to scan every individual's temperature. If the temperature is normal the entry can be provided. This system also scans for the face mask. The face mask detection technique is used to find out whether a person is wearing a mask. It is identical to Object detection.

Firstly, a webcam is used to identify the Face Mask in live video footage. If the mask is detected, then the next step is to check the temperature of the person. If the temperature is ok, then the person is requested to scan their ID card so that their barcode which contains their employee Id is scanned and stored in the DB. The scanned code which contains the unique employee Id is verified by checking the employee Id in the database. If the employee Id is valid, then the person can enter the premises.

This system makes sure all the individuals are following the safety norms and also provides contactless attendance/entry. The below Figure 1 shows a representation of a person with and Without Mask.

Figure 1. With and Without a Mask.

The Structure of the paper is arranged accordingly. The Literature survey and Methodology is described in section II and III. The Methodology is described in detail including all the figures to justify the concepts. The practical results part is given in section IV. Conclusion, References and Future Scope are at the end.

Existing System

"Prevention is better than cure." It is one of the effective measures to prevent the spreading of current viruses in this pandemic era. Many researchers have been doing research on preventing viruses and their cures. At present more than 70% of the population is fully vaccinated. Even vaccinated people are affected by the virus but the recovery rate is very good in vaccinated people than in not vaccinated people. The government is doing its best in a full-paced way to make sure all of the population is fully vaccinated. In these situations, it's better to be self-aware and cautious to prevent the spread of viruses.

In the meantime, many systems have been introduced for face mask detection for the virus.

A Face Mask detection model named "An Automated System to Limit COVID-19 Using Facial Mask Detection in Smart City Network" was proposed by Mohammad Marufur Rahman, Md. Motaleb Hossen Manik, Saifuddin Mahmud, Md. Milon Islam, Jong-Hoon Kim.

These authors proposed a system that restricts the spread of the Corona virus by finding out people who are not wearing or using a face mask. This system detects whether an individual is wearing a mask or not in public places. This system makes use of CCTV cameras to monitor. If a person without wearing a mask is identified, the concerned officials will be informed and they can take the necessary actions. This System uses deep learning and the architecture is trained to detect people with and without masks.

Another Face Mask detection model named "FACE MASK DETECTION USING DEEP LEARNING" was proposed by Ravi Kishore and Rekha - These authors proposed a system that detects if the person is wearing a face mask or not in a live video stream. This system uses machine learning techniques to implement this model. If anyone in the live stream is not wearing a face mask a rectangle is drawn around the face with a dialog entitled "NO MASK" in red color and if a person is wearing a mask, a green color rectangle is drawn around the face with a dialog entitled "MASK DETECTED."

This model is trained in such a way that it can detect if a person is wearing a mask or not accurately. The dataset does not contain any duplicate or morphed images, it is trained with real-time people wearing different kinds of masks with different colors and designs. This model can be deployed at any Organization, Schools, Colleges, etc.

Design Methodology

This Proposed System introduces an automated system for detecting face masks and the temperature of the individual before entering the office premises. The camera is used to detect the face mask and this captured image is fed into the system which goes through a series of steps before identifying the face mask and then detecting the temperature. After these two steps, the person is requested to scan the ID card.

The Proposed System can be divided into two parts/scenarios. Part one consists of the face mask and temperature detection. Part two contains the scanning of ID cards, checking the details in the Database and providing the entry to the employee. Each of these two parts is explained in detail in the below Figure 2 Block Diagram:

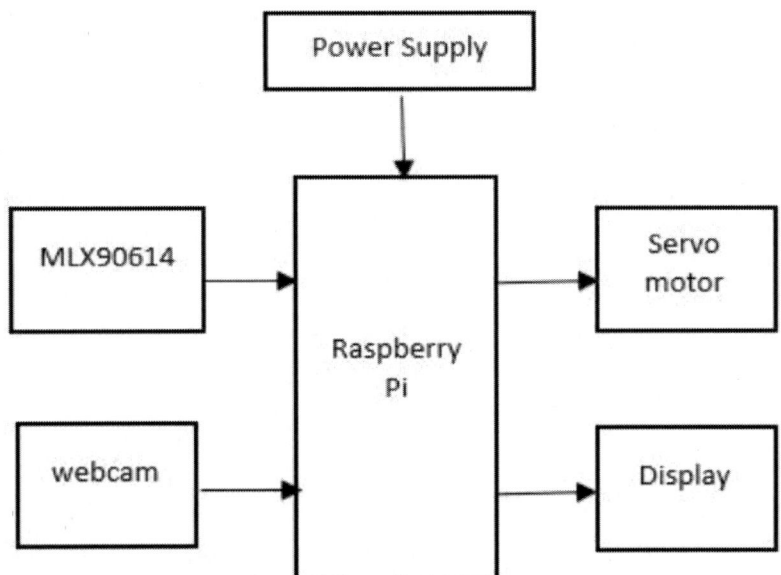

Figure 2. Block Diagram.

Figure 3. Representation of people with masks and without masks.

Face Mask Detection

TensorFlow was used to train the system. It is a free open-source software library for deep learning, artificial intelligence (AI), and machine learning frameworks. It has pre-trained models which can help with image classification using CNN. The below Figure 3 shows the actual representation of people with masks and without masks.

CNN

CNN stands for Convolutional Neural Network. It is an algorithm for Deep learning that can take inputs as images and helps to identify various aspects & objects in the image and differentiate them from one another. Every image in CNN is represented in the form of an array of pixel values. These models help to train as well as test each input image as the image goes through a series of layers, they are:

Convolutional Layer and Pooling Layer which helps in feature extraction. Fully Connected Layer (FC) for classification and SoftMax function is used to classify an object using binary number 1 or 0. The below Figure 4 shows the layers of CNN Algorithm.

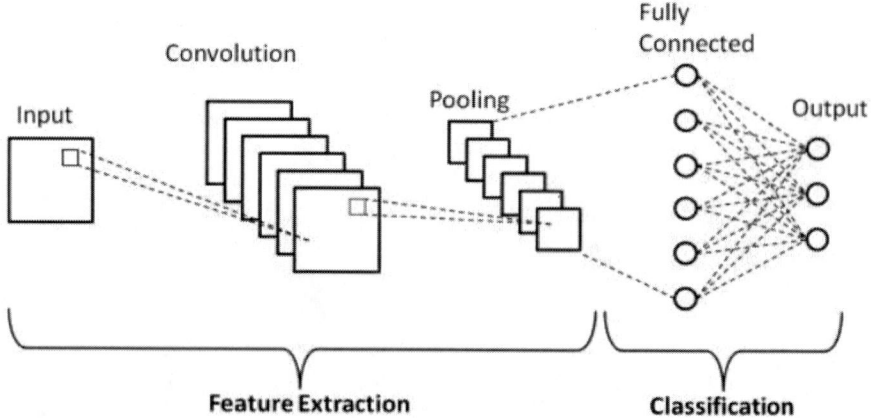

Figure 4. CNN Algorithm.

- Convolutional Layer is used to extract features from the input image and to learn the image. In the activation function of the convolutional layer, the classification layer gives a set of binary numbers 0 or 1, which specifies the class of the object.

- Pooling Layer would help to reduce the no of parameters when the images are too large. The structural size of the convoluted feature is minimized which helps in lowering the computational power that is required in processing the data by reducing the dimensions. Pooling is of two types: Max pooling, and Average pooling. Max Pooling is used to obtain the highest value of a pixel from a part of the image covered by the kernel. It also helps in noise reduction and de-noising. Average Pooling is used to obtain the average of all the values from the part of the image. Max pooling performance is better than compared to Average pooling.

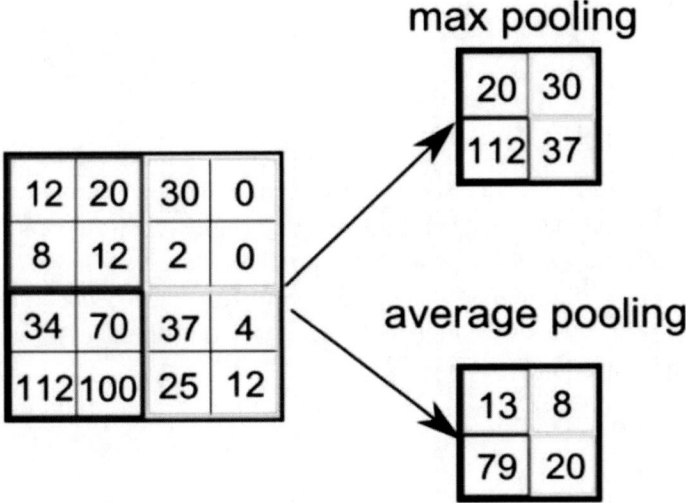

Figure 5. Types of Pooling layer.

- The above Figure 5 shows types of Pooling layer.
- The high-level features defined by the output of the convolutional layer have many combinations.
- A fully Connected Layer is used to learn these non-linear combinations.

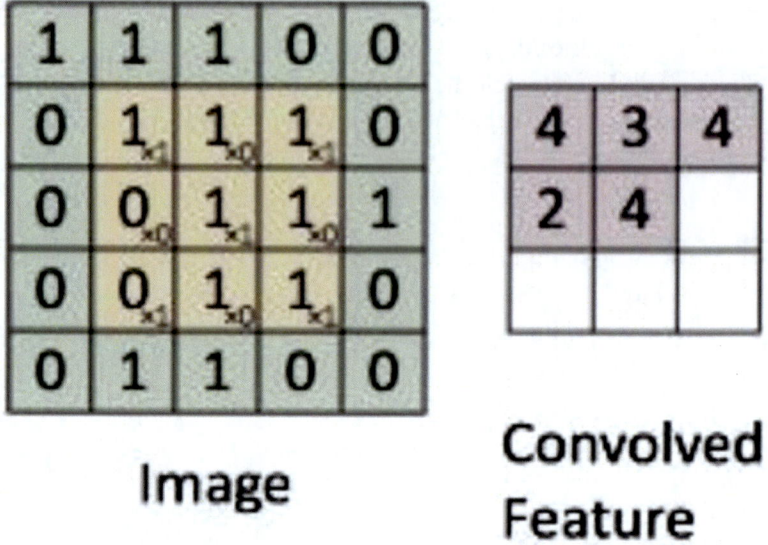

Figure 6. Image converted to convoluted feature.

- The above Figure 6 shows conversion of Image to convoluted feature.
- The flattened image is passed through a feed-forward neural network and later backpropagation is applied for every loop of training. Finally, the model will be able to differentiate between higher and lower levels of features in the images and further classify them using the SoftMax approach.

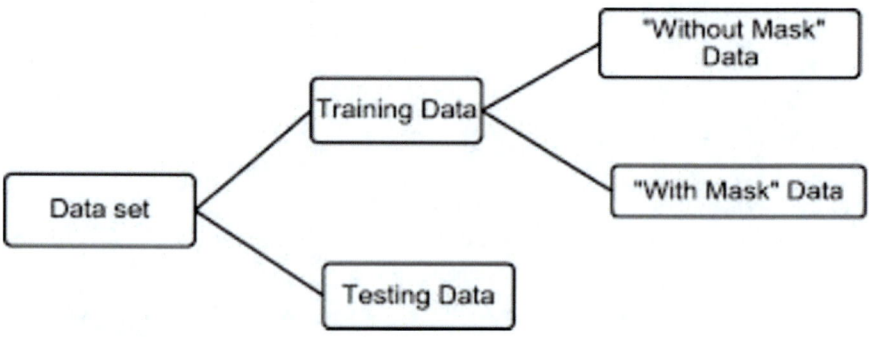

Figure 7. Data Set.

- The above Figure 7 shows Data set which contains Training and Testing data.

Detection of Temperature

The MLX90614 is a thermometer for the *contactless temperature* measure of any object's temperature. The sensor uses Infra-Red rays to detect the temperature of an object without making any interaction with the object. I2C protocol is used to communicate with the microcontroller. The MLX90614 sensor is calibrated in the range of -40 °C to 125 °C for the ambient temperature and for the object temperature it is -70 °C to 382.2 °C.

Stefan-Boltzmann Law is used here, it states that Infrared Energy is emitted by all living beings and objects and the intensity of the emitted energy will be directly proportional to the temperature of the same object. The amount of IR energy emitted from any object/thing is used to calculate the temperature of the object.

The sensor can be directly interfaced with a microcontroller without any external components. The Vdd and Gnd pins are used for the power supply(5V). For optimum EMC and filtering noise, the capacitor can be used. SCL and SDA are signal pins that are used for communication which is the I2C protocol.

Providing Attendance and Entry

In this model, Zbar/PyZbar is used to read barcodes. It is an open-source software package for scanning and reading barcodes from different sources like images, video streams, raw intensity sensors, etc. It can be used with Python Programming as a library to detect the barcodes. In this model, a webcam is used as input, from which the barcode can be scanned and processed to verify the barcode.

After scanning the ID card, the scanned barcode is verified in the database, If the details are present in the database, the gates are opened and the person can enter into premises. If the data is not present in the database, the person is requested to contact the helpdesk for further assistance.

Vaccination Status

This model can also display the vaccination status of the person if necessary. The scanned barcode is verified in the database and the Vaccination status also can be retrieved.

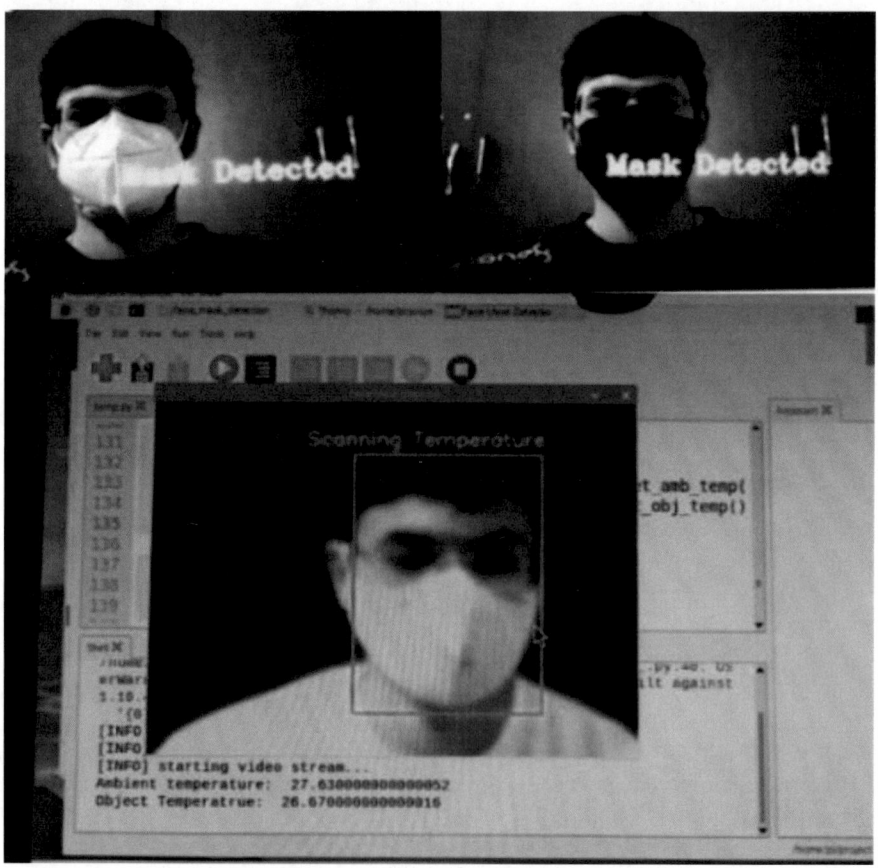

Figure 8. Face Mask detection and temperature scanning.

Results

When a person arrives at the gate first, they are checked for the Face Mask using the webcam. If the mask is present, then the temperature of the person is checked without any contact. If the temperature is normal, they are requested to scan their Identity Card. The system scans the barcode on the ID card and checks the barcode number with the database. If the number is present in the database, then the entry is successful. Gates are opened to allow the person into the premises.

If the person is not wearing the face mask, he/she is requested to wear a mask. If the temperature of the person is not normal, he is requested to proceed according to the management guidelines. If the Scanned ID card is not found in the database, then the person is requested to contact the helpdesk for further assistance. In any of the false scenarios, the person is requested to proceed accordingly with the desired message viewed on the display.

The following figures show the system outputs of Face mask detection, Temperature scanning (Figure 8), if the mask is detected or not (Figure 9), ID card scanning (Figures 10 and 11).

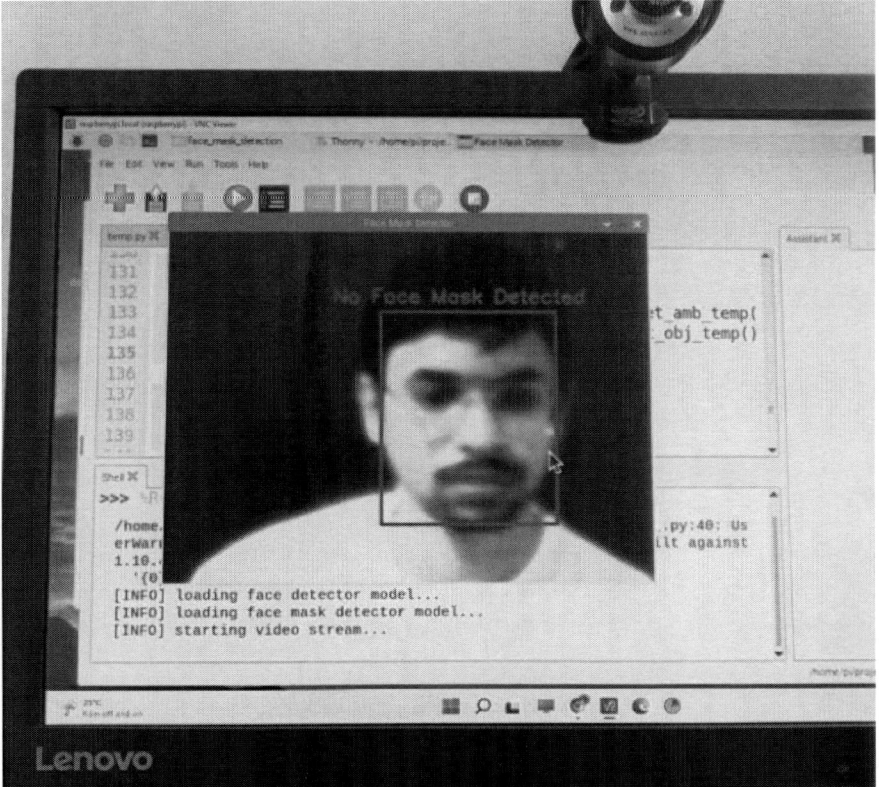

Figure 9. No Face Mask Detected.

Figure 10. ID card scanning to enter the premises.

Figure 11. Scanned ID card.

Conclusion

With the aid of advancing technology, many efforts are made to contribute to public healthcare and welfare management. This system is a part of this contribution to the health care system. A successful system with a more efficient and accurate model for the detection of face mask, temperature and contactless entry system is achieved. This model can be used in many low and high computational scenarios. The dataset has many robust features and has been trained in many variations giving a large varied and augmented dataset which helps the system to identify different types of masks making it more accurate and efficient. By using Keras TensorFlow, OpenCV, Python and CNN this model achieved its efficiency and accuracy.

Future Scope

This system does not only focus on detecting the face mask. It is focused on multiple aspects compared to other proposed systems. This model helps to beat the common limitations of the other proposed models. As attendance/timesheet entry is mandatory at every organization/company, this model can be used at all organizations. This model can be extended with other parameters such as maintaining social distance, sanitization, etc. These aspects depend on the severity of the situation and can be implemented when it's necessary. This can also be used to register the number of people going in and out of the premises.

Finally, the proposed model is able to achieve its goals with more efficiency and accuracy.

References

Abdul Subhani Shaik, Ram Kumar Karsh, Mohiul Islam, Surendra Pal Singh, "A Secure and Robust Autoencoder-Based Perceptual Image Hashing for Image Authentication," *Wireless Communications and Mobile Computing*, vol. 2022, Article ID 1645658, 17 pages, 2022. https://doi.org/10.1155/2022/1645658.

Kavya preethi D., K. Sowmya sri, M. Mani Venkata, G. Krishna sai – *Computer Science & Engineering: "Automatic Temperature Scanner and Face Mask Detection using IOT."*

https://pyimagesearch.com/2020/05/04/covid-19-face-mask-detector-with-opencv-keras-tensorflow-and-deep-learning.

Hiten Goyal, Karanveer Sidana, Charanjeet Singh, Abhilasha Jain & Swathi Jindal - *A real-time face mask detection system using Convolutional Neural Network – 2022*.

Merugu, S., Jain, K., Mittal, A., Raman, B., "Sub-scene Target Detection and Recognition Using Deep Learning Convolution Neural Networks," *Lecture Notes in Electrical Engineering*, 2020, Vol. 601-Issue, PP-1082-1101.

Michael J. Jones, Paul Viola Robust Real-Time Face Detection, *International Journal of Computer Vision* 57, 2004.

Mohammad Rahman, Saifuddin Mahmud, Md. Motaleb Hossen Manik, Md. Milon Islam, Jong Hoon Kim – *Computer Science: "An Automated System to Limit COVID-19 Using Facial Mask Detection in Smart City Network."*

Ms. Sonal Dhuldhaj, M. A. Khan - *Contactless Attendance System in COVID-19 scenario july 2021*.

Multi-angle Head Pose Classification when wearing the Mask for Face Recognition under the COVID-19 Coronavirus Epidemic in 2020 International Conference on High-Performance Big Data and Intelligence Systems (IEEE, 2020).

Sneha Sakshi, Ajay Kumar Gupta, Uttam Kumar, Sudeept Singh Yadav – *"Face Mask Detection System using CNN."*

Susanto Susanto, Febri Alwan Putra, Riska Analia, Ika Karlina Laila Nur Suciningtyas - *The Face Mask Detection for Preventing the Spread of COVID-19 at Politeknik Negeri Batam – 2021*.

Chapter 3

Stock Market Analysis and Prediction Using Long Short Term Memory 6+

Padmavathi Nayak[*], BTech
Hitaarth Jainn, BTech
Gouri Shetty Ramesh, ME
Jammula Srini, BTech
and Bandarwar Shruthika

Department of Computer Science and Engineering, Vallurupalli Nageswara Rao Vignana Jyothi Institute of Engineering & Technology, Hyderabad, India

Abstract

Stock market is a highly volatile form of investment. The organizations make money by allowing the people or the shareholders to buy the parts of their company. They involve the shareholders in the important decisions and earn money through gains and dividend. The analysis of stock market helps in clever and thoughtful investment and hence brings heavy returns on investment. Though the involvement of many factors makes it nearly impossible to predict the patterns of the stock price, we can predict the patterns to some accuracy using the historical data and estimating the future data using statistical models. This functionality of dropping the very historic values according to the dataset can be done by LSTM. The comparison of this method with other methods like Random Forest Classification, SVM, etc., adds as a benchmark check to the same. Our literature review's initial goal has been to ascertain if the historical prices of the stocks could be used to predict the future stock prices (R,

---

[*] Corresponding Author's Email: padmavathinayak12@gmail.com.

In: Information and Knowledge Systems
Editors: Manaswini Pradhan and Satchidananda Dehurl
ISBN: 979-8-89113-303-7
© 2024 Nova Science Publishers, Inc.

Nandakumar, Uttamraj, K. R., Vishal, R., & Lokeswari, Y. V., 2018). The Kim and Ingoo paper Han had the ANN optimization introduced with GA (Kim, Kyoung-jae and Ingoo Han, 2000). A stochastic global optimization algorithm is the genetic algorithm The GA algorithm is an algorithm that is evolutionary in nature, it makes use of binary representations based on mutations and re-combinations for the optimization. Specifically, it is the most recent synthesis that integrates the theory and a knowledge of genetics.

To verify stock market forecasts, Hassan employed the Hidden Markov Model (Hassan M. R. and Nath B., 2005). Another paper (Venugopal Deneshkumar, Kaliyaperumal Senthamarai Kannan and Niraikulathan Sonai Muthu) attempted the Hidden Markov Model. A statistical model called a Hidden Markov Model (HMM) is employed in machine learning. It can be used to explain how external, indirectly observable causes influence the evolution of observable occurrences. We can forecast a series of unknown variables using this class of probabilistic graphical models by using a collection of observed variables. The observations are thought to be independent of the other variables, which is how it operated. To forecast the price of bitcoin, Sean and Simon used RNN (McNally S., Roche J. and S. Caton, 2018). Concept of RNN was also used in another research. The Multilayer Perceptron (MLP) has been used by several academics to anticipate stock prices (H. White, 1988; Y. Yoon and G. Swales, 1991). The MLP, however, only examines a single observation at a time. Indicators like the Simple Moving Average have been used in numerous articles in recent years. The MLP, however, only analyses one observation at a time (Kudipudi, Srinivas, Subba Rao Polamuri and A. Krishna Mohan, 2020). Concept of Artificial Neural Networks have been implemented but the 'black box' feature of the model has been an obstruction (Deshmukh, Yogita, Saratkar Deepmala and Tiwari Yash, 2019; V Papineni, Swarajya Lakshmi Mallikarjuna Reddy A, Sudeepti yarlagadda, Snigdha Yarlagadda, and Haritha Akkineni, 2021). Indicators like the Simple Moving Average (SMA) have been used in numerous articles recently for machine learning tasks (Wang, Yanshan. 2014; S. Lauren and S. D. Harlili, 2014). MA) for challenges involving machine learning (Wang, Yanshan. 2014; S. Lauren and S. D. Harlili, 2014). The methods of SVM, Random Forest were also used and compared to standard methods, but the accuracy was a bit low (Lee, Ming-Chi. 2009; Thakur, Manoj, and Deepak Kumar. 2018; Vijh, Mehar, Deeksha Chandola, Vinay Anand Tikkiwal, Arun Kumar, 2020; Kranthi Sai Reddy, V, 2018). After deciding to use the LSTM neural network to make stock forecasts, time series data is collected from stock firm prices of the stock and related macro economic variables over a period of 1 year (V papineni, Swarajya Lakshmi, 2021; Kudipudi, Sriniva, Subba Rao Polamuri and A. Krishna Mohan, 2020).

Stock Market Analysis and Prediction Using Long Short Term Memory

Keywords: SVM-Support Vector Machine, LSTM-Long Short-term Memory, random forest classification, stock market analysis

Introduction

Acceptance of machine learning in the financial industry has encouraged more use and a wider range of factors that may be assessed and predicted for sound business decisions. There are numerous ways to forecast and analyse stock marketdata for more informed decision-making. The model may trainon a vast quantity of data for analysis and prediction, but the main cause of the model's lower accuracy has been the presenceof a larger noise-to-clean-data ratio.

The created model will attempt to reduce noise to the greatest extent feasible and will assist in forecasting the values for the nth day the user requests. The dynamic dashboard will help theconsumer better comprehend the data so that they may make better data-driven decisions rather than assumptions-driven ones. This project aims at good accuracy for informed decisions.

A successful stock forecast can result in enormous gains for the seller and the broker. The predictions made in stock market are mostly very random which proves that they can be done correctly if we invest some time and analysis into it. This method ensures that the accuracy of the data is improved and the user can make informed decisions. A lot of study has been drawn to the application of machine learning to stock predictionbecause of its effective and precise measures. One of the main constituent of machine learning is the dataset. The correctness of the dataset is very necessary for the results and analysis to be accurate to a certain percent as a small change in data means a huge change in the result. We have performed machine learningon a dataset. The dataset is taken from Yahoo Finance and has the basic attributes. The data is very much based on the daily transactions happening throughout the world. The model is then tested using the testing data. For this hypothesis, both LSTM and regression models are used individually. Regression includes reducing error, and LSTM helps with long-term memory retention of the data and findings. Last but not least, the graphs for price variations with dates (regression-based models) and between actual and expected pricing.

LSTM Literature Review in Stock Market Price Prediction

Numerous academics and investors have examined the stock market's data. According to the numerous papers, some studiesemployed tree-based models to estimate share return, while others used deep learning to produce future share values. Someresearchers additionally employed the Adaboost algorithm. Economists have explored a wide range of tactics used to "beat"the market since the early days of the stock market. The stock market has shown to be impossible to "beat." However, asimple task because economists continue to look for ways to achieve it today. The Google Trend data utilised for this research has given all types of economists a new weapon to tryand subvert the market. Data analytics have started to question why as more academic institutions (Boston University/Warwick Business School) and major organisations (ESPN) have used this trend data in their study. The simplicity with which this analytical data may be studied and presented helps to explain the recent increase in interest in it. SVM was present during several processes. Only the training and testing on the same data were used in these articles. Only historical data was used in the procedure, and only past values were used to make the prediction. In order to make comparisons, prior values have been predicted.

Prediction of the data pattern for the future has not been completed. The future value of the portfolio for the given company has been forecasted by our model using historical data, which also captured the trend. The informationis highly concrete and is very helpful for discovering relationships. This makes it possible for those who are lookingat the data to determine whether or not their data comparison isgenuinely relevant. The ambition of economists to always look for new ways to subvert the market is another factor contributing to the increased demand for this knowledge. This is a constant because successful economists will always seek out novel approaches to data analysis and trend detection.

LSTM Networks

LSTM can read between the intermediate layer. It is the main advantage of the algorithm. Without the activation function, the data can be retained for a stipulated amount of time. Long Short Term Memory Networks, also called "LSTMs," is a specific type of RNN supporting learn long-term dependencies while rejecting old input. Since they were created, they have been improved upon and made more widely known. They are currently widely utilised in many areas of statistical analysis and have given good results with many various spread of data. Issues of sequence prediction can be leant by LSTM.

The sequence of inputs is not fixed but they have an input sequencewhich can be taken into consideration along with the contextual information to generate an output sequence (Bengio, Y., P. Simard, and P. Frasconi. 1994). Hence, the LSTM proves to be very helpful for the same. The model may have trouble remembering information that spans over a longer period if the main pattern is lost or if the trend underfitting occurs. Therefore, when producing predictions in accordance, LSTM ensures that the long term data is removed from its memory. Unlike the RNN, which has a similar structure as illustrated in Figure 1, the many LSTM layers have unique structures. These elements come together in a unique way to provide the answerto the long-term memory challenge.

This solves the problem of perishable gradient. As the data stored in the cell is converted in a non-recurring manner causing the gradient not to end when the distribution happens backwards (R, Nandakumar Uttamraj, K. R., Vishal, R., & Lokeswari, Y. V., 2018).

For the memory of the project, use LSTM. We use it as it is more efficient than the regular neural networks. The reason why they perform so good is that they are very adept at remembering the patterns very well. The necessary information is used and retained while the unnecessary data is dumped and gotten rid of as illustrated in Figure 2.

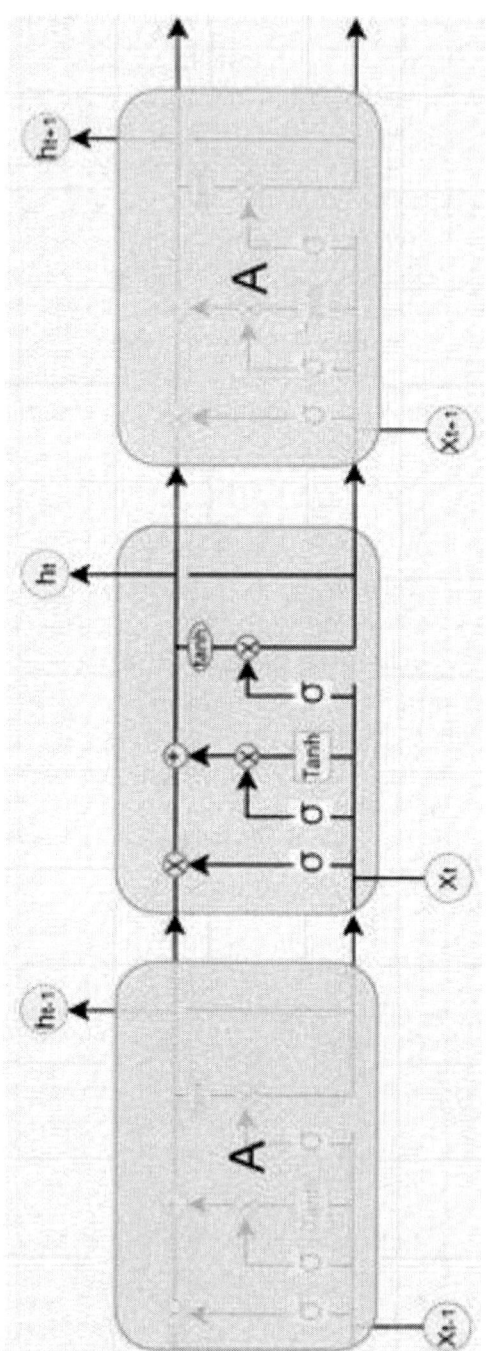

Figure 1. The repeating layer of LSTM having four layers.

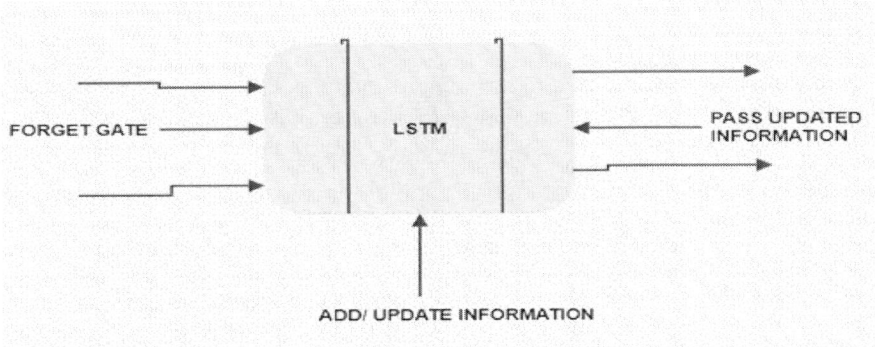

Figure 2. LSTM gates and purposes of the gates.

1. REMOVE Gate
This gate decides what data can be retained and what data can be dumped off from each cell state. The two inputs are the present information and the penultimate information. These 2 inputs were provided to the LSTM.

2. INPUT Gate
The INPUT gate decides which information and data is important and which information is not important. This gate is necessary for the network to remember the data which is required.

3. CELL State
The necessary information gathered helps in defining the new cell state. The cell state is multiplied by the output of the forget state. The values are updated such that the loss of data is less and the network is viable and accurate for the results that can be depended upon to make a decision.

4. OUTPUT Gate
The next hidden state is declared by the output gate. This is thegate which comes last. The passing freshly updated cell decides what information the hidden state should comprise of.

 LSTM has been used in various domains and fields whenever the data had to be forgotten or ignored after a certain period oftime. This algorithm has found very good application in robotics, music composition, time series data prediction etc. The data is to be cleaned properly for the same to have proper accuracy.

The LSTM has been used by applications like Google to develop applications.

The memory cell referred to as the cell state plays an importantrole in the LSTM model. It makes sure that the preservation ofthe state over the time happens. The LSTMS are given the fullknowledge of what is happening before the state and after the state. LSTM handles noise very well and the back propagation error isrectified to a very huge extent. The generalization power of LSTM is very good.

Figure 3 illustrates the dataflow in the network and how the tanhfunctions work. It depicts the various works of the network and the numerous gates present too.

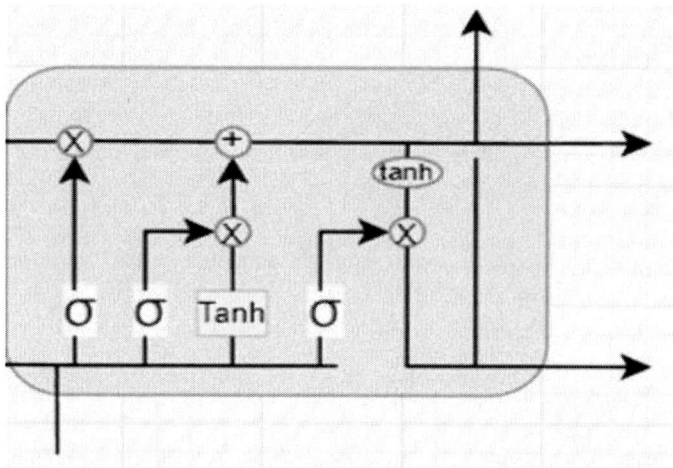

Figure 3. Data Flow in the network.

Proposed Work

Dataset Details:

For the dataset, we took the data to be dynamic in nature. We obtained the dataset from the yahoo finance dataset which is updated live. The data was fetched using a command and addedinto the notebook. The data was imported for Apple, Google, Microsoft and Amazon. We mainly worked on this data. The data contains all the values of opening prices, Day high value, Day low value, Closing value and Date for one year from the date the execution is done.

The data hence had entries depending on the absence of weekends and had 5 columns. The image illustrated in Figure 2 describes the data and the attributes of the data. The data has the following attributes:

1. Closing stock value: The quantity of unsold items still in the company's possession as of a particular date is referred to as closing stock. In other words, it is possible to say that this is stock that is currently beingused and is awaiting sale.
2. Opening stock value: It is the amount of valuables at the beginning of the time of accounting that the company keeps with it. The value is in compliance with the standards of accounting.
3. High Value: The maximum amount at which a company traded throughout the day of business is known as the "today's high," which is often more thanthe "close price" or similar to the "opening price."
4. Low Value: Low value is the value of trading which ismostly the lowest point in the trade of the company forthat particular day.

The steps taken are given in the table 1 in the form of an algorithm as shown in Figure 5. The algorithm involves various steps like the loading of data as illustrated in Figure 4, importing necessary libraries, training the model usingthe training data and testing the model for its performance usingthe testing data.

Table 1. The usage of each level of the algorithm of data processing

Step No.	Task Name	Description
1.	Load the dataset	Dataset was loaded from yahoo finance.
2.	Import Libraries	Libraries like tensorflow, yfinance, sklearn, pandas.numpy were imported.
3.	Data Pre-processing	The preprocessing was done by adding the end date to shares, standardizing the data.
4.	Training and testingsplit of data	The data was split for the raining and testing of the model.
5.	LSTM Model	The model for LSTM was defined with timesteps and features given along with the regressor model in one of the layers to allow predictability of the future values.

Table 1. (Continued)

Step No.	Task Name	Description
6.	Prediction of the model	The data is predicted according to the number of days given by the user accordingly.
7.	Plotting the data	The pattern of the predictions of the past and the future are plotted together. This graph helps the user to see if the prediction is acting as an outlier or is following the pattern.
8.	Dynamic dashboard	The dashboard is plotted for the easy understanding and deciphering of the data. This dashboard helps to reduce the amount of confusion and helps in improving understandability of the results. It satisfies the aim of good decision making by giving a certain level of comfort to the user.

The last part focuses on user perspective to show the ease with which the data can be understood and the result can be deciphered.

We use the previous data for the training part where the data is captured, patterns are recognized, model is built and the data is trained for the predictions. Then the comparison has been done with Random Forest, SV M etc. The data Random Forest Algorithm makes sure that the decision is not wholly dependent on the single decision tree but is averaged from many decision trees to keep the decisions accurate to a certain rate. Support vector machine or the SVM is utilized to take care of the Classification problems and is a supervised learning algorithm.

The decision boundary also called the best line of fit can be divided into classes. This division helps us to easily classify data in the coming time period. This line or boundary is called the optimal decision boundary.

[ ]

Date	Open	High	Low	Close	Adj Close	\
2021-08-23	148.309998	150.190002	147.889999	149.710007	148.875778	
2021-08-24	149.449997	150.860001	149.149994	149.619995	148.786270	
2021-08-25	149.809998	150.320007	147.800003	148.360001	147.533279	
2021-08-26	148.350006	149.119995	147.509995	147.539993	146.717865	
2021-08-27	147.479996	148.750000	146.830002	148.600006	147.771957	
...	...	...	...	...	...	
2022-08-15	171.520004	173.389999	171.350006	173.190002	173.190002	
2022-08-16	172.779999	173.710007	171.660004	173.029999	173.029999	
2022-08-17	173.750000	176.149994	172.570007	174.550003	174.550003	
2022-08-18	173.750000	174.899994	173.119995	174.149994	174.149994	
2022-08-19	173.029999	173.740005	171.309998	171.520004	171.520004	

Date	Volume	Dates
2021-08-23	60131800	2021-08-23
2021-08-24	48606400	2021-08-24
2021-08-25	58991300	2021-08-25
2021-08-26	48597200	2021-08-26
2021-08-27	55802400	2021-08-27
...	...	...
2022-08-15	54091700	2022-08-15
2022-08-16	56377100	2022-08-16
2022-08-17	79542000	2022-08-17
2022-08-18	62290100	2022-08-18
2022-08-19	70211500	2022-08-19

[251 rows x 7 columns]

Figure 4. The data snippet showing the various attributes.

The diagram given below explains the flow of process control in the project. The algorithm passes through the various phasesof machine learning. Diagram illustrating the machine learning process used to evaluate the effectiveness of each algorithm under test. The "Learning dataset" and the "Independent test set" are the initial subsets that are created for each dataset.

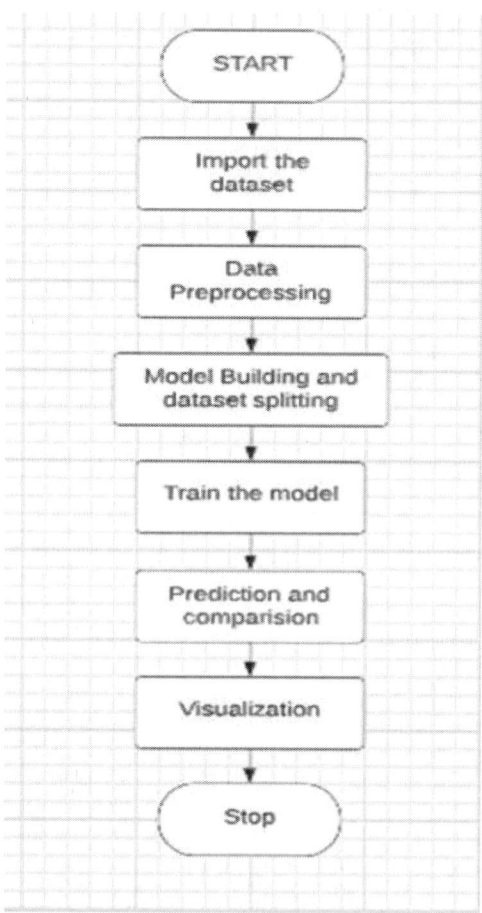

Figure 5. The algorithm of data processing.

The libraries imported are tensorflow, keras, numpy, pandas, plotly. Each of them have been used for the respective purposes. The basic use of TensorFlow is to neural networks and inference related jobs. It is cost free and can be used to apply for a varied range of tasks. It is easily available for the variety of tasks in the statistical world.

The Keras is used by the analysts for various tasks and is available cost-free. It mostly finds application in artificial neural networks. TensorFlow, Microsoft Cognitive Toolkit, Theano, and PlaidML were just a few of the backends that Keras supported up until version 2.3.

Numpy supports arrays and all its types including the large arrays which have many dimensions. It can also perform many operations on the arrays too.

In order to extract meaningful information from this raw data and feed it into the training model for successful decisions and diagnoses, data preparation is very necessary. The methods illustrated in table show the use of each level and how the models can be built quickly using the same.

Discussion

On applying the LSTM model to the dataset, we found that different accuracies were a result of different epochs and batchsizes. The data was cleaned and pre-processed to ensure better performance of dataset for accurate results.

The data used is depicted on a graph in Figure 6.

The graph shows the data points in the dataset jotted as a line chart. It is used to find the trend in the data until now and can be used by the user for analysis of the data that is historical. It contains the data of around one year for the company.

Figure 6. The graphical representation of the dataset data points.

```
1/1 [==============================] - 0s 20ms/step
        Close                  Dates
0  169.231934  2022-08-22 04:33:16.598533
1  171.259888  2022-08-23 04:33:16.598533
2  169.529587  2022-08-24 04:33:16.598533
3  173.382065  2022-08-25 04:33:16.598533
4  170.820175  2022-08-26 04:33:16.598533
```

Figure 7. The prediction of data for the future 5 days.

We even predicted the value of the data for the stock share after 5 days using LSTM as depicted in Figure 7. The past data has been used in a recurring format to get the data for the future prediction. The snapshot of the result shows the data share value predictions for day1, day2,.....day n till the user specified day.

The highest accuracy we achieved was 97.7% as depicted in Figure 8. The data was different for different epochs and the accuracy was also different. We got the highest accuracy and least loss of data for the given epoch after comparing for all the data with the actual value.

The dynamic dashboard of the data along with future trends and past data has been constructed using plotly as can be seen in Figure 9.

The dynamic dashboard in Figure 9 embodies the user friendliness by giving the data date wise and the data can be read once the user moves the mouse pointer towards the line. The red line in the end of the chart shows the data predicted for the future. It is observed how the data fits in the trend and uses the past data at a restricted extent to predict the future values.

The comparison accuracies with other standard algorithms are shown in Table 2.

Table 2. Result Comparison

Method used	Accuracy
K- Nearest Neighbors	0.59
Long Short TermMemory	0.97
Random Forest	0.65
Support Vector Machine	0.51

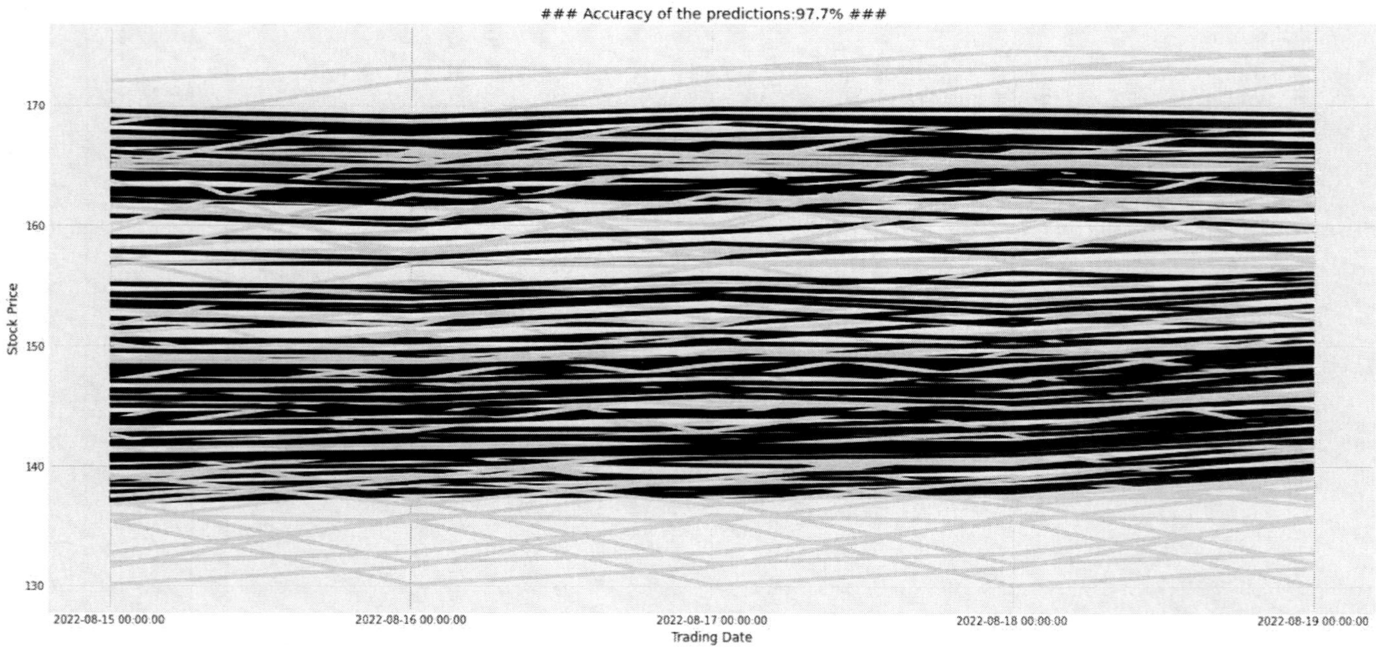

Accuracy of the predictions:97.7%

Figure 8. The graph of testing accuracies.

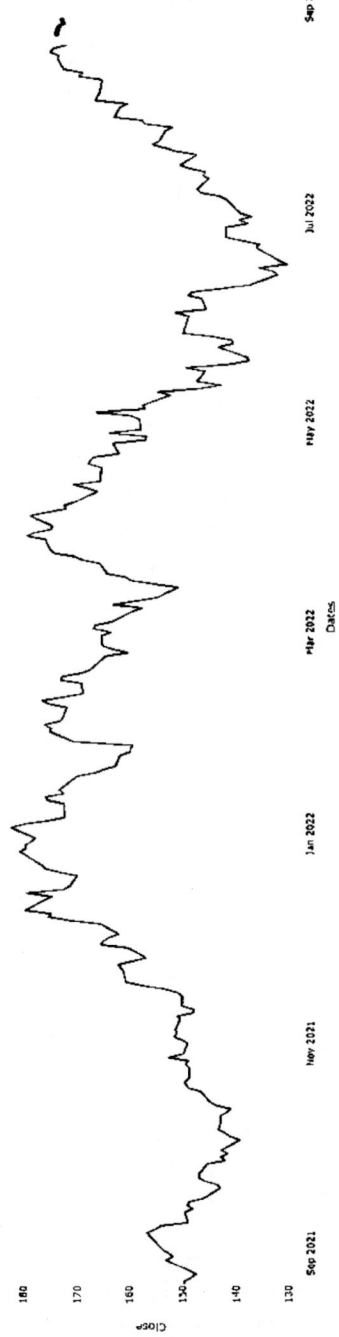

Figure 9. Dynamic graph of historical and predicted data.

The dashboard is such that it has images organized such that they can give pictorial representation of images in a user friendly and deciphering way. This dashboard contains the dataof the historical values represented in blue and the future predictions until the date specified by the user.

Conclusion

In terms of stock market data prediction, this study is an effort to increase the accuracy of data value predictions. The project has demonstrated the superiority of LSTM over alternative algorithms, and data has been accurately forecasted for future dates specified by the user. In order to further improve accuracyand gain a thorough understanding of how the parameters affectshare value and by how much, we want to add more characteristics to the existing model. The same LSTM model can be used with different data from other companies and for other lengths of time. The LSTM Model has performed better than the other models due to the concept of Long Short Term Memory wherein the model is trained to forget the past data trends and remember the most recent trends and have the benefit of the time series. LSTM has been proven to be extremely effective for the sequence prediction and it is so because LSTM can store past information and forget the information that is deemed unnecessary.

Disclaimer

None.

References

Bengio Y., P. Simard, and P. Frasconi. 1994. "Learning Long-Term Dependencies with Gradient Descent Is Difficult." *IEEE Transactions on Neural Networks* 5 (2): 157–66. https://doi.org/10.1109/72.279181.

Deshmukh Yogita, Saratkar Deepmala, Tiwari Yash 2019, "Stock Market Prediction Using Machine Learning," *IJARCCE* 8(1):31-35, January 2019.

Hassan M. R. and Nath B. 2005, "Stock Market Forecasting Using Hidden Markov Model: A New Approach," *5th International Conference on Intelligent Systems Design and Applications* (ISDA'05), 2005.

Kim, Kyoung-jae, and Ingoo Han. 2000. "Genetic Algorithms Approach to Feature Discretization in Artificial Neural Networks for the Prediction of Stock Price Index." *Expert Systems with Applications* 19 (2): 125–32. https://doi.org/10.1016/s0957-4174(00)00027-0.

Kranthi Sai Reddy, V., 2018,"Stock Market Prediction Using Machine Learning," *International Research Journal of Engineering and Technology*, Volume: 05, October 2018.

Kudipudi, Srinivas, Subba Rao Polamuri, A. Krishna Mohan, 2020, *"A Survey on Stock Market Prediction Using Machine Learning Techniques,"* Lecture Notes in Electrical Engineering 601, Springer Link, ICDSMLA 2019 (pp.923-931).

Lauren S. and S. D. Harlili, 2014. "Stock trend prediction using simple moving average supported by news classification," *Advanced Informatics: Concept Theory and Application (ICAICTA) 2014 International Conference of IEEE*, pp. 135- r139, 2014.

Lee, Ming-Chi. 2009. "Using Support Vector Machine with a Hybrid Feature Selection Method to the Stock Trend Prediction." *Expert Systems with Applications* 36 (8): 10896–904. https://doi.org/10.1016/j.eswa.2009.02.038.

McNally S., Roche J. and S. Caton, 2018. "Predicting the price of bitcoin using machine learning," *Proc. 26th Euromicro Int. Conf. Parallel Distrib. Network-Based Process.* (PDP), pp. 339- 343, Mar. 2018.

Nandakumar R., Uttamraj, K. R., Vishal, R., & Lokeswari, Y. V., 2018. "Stock price prediction using long short term memory." *International Research Journal of Engineering and Technology*, 5(03).

Papineni V., Swarajya lakshmi, Mallikarjuna Reddy A., Sudeepti yarlagadda, Snigdha Yarlagadda, and Haritha Akkineni. 2021. "An Extensive Analytical Approach on Human Resources Using Random Forest Algorithm." *International Journal of Engineering Trends and Technology* 69(5):119-27. https://doi.org/10.14445/22315381/ijett-v69i5p217.

Papineni V., Swarajya Lakshmi, Snigdha Yarlagadda, Harita Akkineni, and Mallikarjuna Reddy A. 2021. "Big Data Analytics Applying the Fusion Approach of Multicriteria Decision Making with Deep Learning Algorithms." *International Journal of Engineering Trends and Technology* 69(1): 24-28. https://doi.org/10.14445/22315381/ijett-v69i1p204.

Thakur, Manoj, and Deepak Kumar. 2018. "A Hybrid Financial Trading Support System Using Multi-Category Classifiers and Random Forest." *Applied Soft Computing* 67 (June): 337–49. https://doi.org/10.1016/j.asoc.2018.03.006.

Venugopal Deneshkumar, Kaliyaperumal Senthamarai Kannan and Niraikulathan Sonai Muthu, "Stock Market Trend Prediction Using Hidden Markov Model," *Forecasting in Mathematics - Recent Advances, New Perspectives and Applications* Publisher: Intechopen.

Vijh, Mehar, Deeksha Chandola, Vinay Anand Tikkiwal, Arun Kumar, 2020, "Stock Closing Price Prediction using Machine Learning Techniques," *Procedia Computer Science*, Volume 167(pp. 599-606), 2020.

Wang, Yanshan. 2014. "Stock Price Direction Prediction by Directly Using Prices Data: An Empirical Study on the KOSPI and HSI." *International Journal of Business Intelligence and Data Mining* 9 (2): 145. https://doi.org/10.1504/ijbidm.2014.065091.

White H., 1988, "Economic prediction using neural networks: Thecase of ibm daily stock returns," *Neural Networks 1988. IEEE International Conference* on, pp. 451-458, 1988.

Yoon Y. and G. Swales,1991 "Predicting stock price performance: A neural network approach." *System Sciences 1991. Proceedings of the Twenty-Fourth Annual Hawaii International Conference* on, vol. 4, pp. 156-162.

Chapter 4

Network Anomaly Detection Using a Random Forest Classifier

T. Subburaj[1]
K. Srujan Raju[2]
N. M. Sinchana[3]
K. Suthendran[4]
and Voruganti Naresh Kumar[5]

[1]Department of Master of Computer Applications, RajaRajeswari College of Engineering, Bangalore, India
[2]Department of Computer Science and Engineering, CMR Technical Campus, Hydrapad, India
[3]Department of Information Science and Engineering, RajaRajeswari College of Engineering, Bangalore, India
[4]Department of Information Technology, Kalasalingam Academy of Research and Education, Tamilnadu, India
[5]Department of Computer Science and Engineering, CMR Technical Campus, Hydrapad, India

Abstract

Machine Learning (ML), which is a sub-section of Artificial Intelligence (AI) which lets in all kinds of programs to emerge as greater way at predicting consequences without being explicitly programmed to do so. ML algorithms use historic records to predict new outputs. Classical device getting to know is frequently categorized with the aid of using how a set of rules learns to grow to be extra correct in its predictions. Network-attacks are looking to be more complex, displaying more problems in accurately recognizing anomalies, and the inability to avert these anomalies may compromise security services' credibility.

In: Information and Knowledge Systems
Editors: Manaswini Pradhan and Satchidananda Dehurl
ISBN: 979-8-89113-303-7
© 2024 Nova Science Publishers, Inc.

Signature-based Intrusion Detection Systems (SIDS) and Anomaly-based Intrusion Detection Systems (AIDS) are the two types of Intrusion Detection Systems (IDS). The framework is sorely tested with the new Test and Train data set. There are many applications for random forests. Probability estimation and prediction have been done using it. Infiltrator detection has yet to be automated with the technique, though. Detecting anomalies with Random Forests Algorithm is a key component of our proposed system.

Keywords: machine learning, decision tree, random forest, anomaly, SIDS, AIDS

Introduction

Cyber-attacks are getting more complex day by day, posing more hurdles in detecting intrusions effectively, and failure to prevent intrusions could jeopardise security services cred- ibility. An Intrusion Detection System (IDS) is a device or software program which looks onto malicious acts or policy breaking on a network system. By making use of a confidential information and event management system, any malicious acts or violation can be reported or collected on a central network (Yasir Hamid et al., 2016).

Computer safety is to be considered as a crucial issue which is a result of the continuous development of business in agile manner, and the growth of the cyber communities. Network intrusion detection techniques are critical for preventing ma- liciousbehaviour in our system and network. An Intrusion Detection System is a collection of both types of program that examines a whether there are any malicious activities present in the system. The security breaches are identified frequently by safety and event management. There are many IDS that can identify the intrusions very quickly.

Signature-based IDS looks for the things and a form of pattern in computer system, for example byte sequences, or known dangerous attacks patterns that the malware will use, to find out the possible threats. The term "signature" was actually formed by an antivirus software, which is predominantly recognized as signatures. The rather usage in signature-based IDS is that it has the ability to quickly identify and recognize pre-defined attacks, new intrusions are hard to detect because it contains new pattern that cannot be understood by the network system (Praneet Singh et al., 2021).

Many IDSs nowadays are rule-based systems, indicating that their performance is heavily reliant based on the regulations under-lined by security

Network Anomaly Detection Using a Random Forest Classifier

experts. The process of encoding rules is expensive and lengthy due to the large amount of network traffic. Using a rule-driven language that is specified, security personnel must manually alter or deploy new rules. The identification of these intrusions in real time is a significant topic in the networking field in order to maintain user anonymity and trust.

Problem Statement

Attacks are just a few of the sorts of threats that damage ahuge number of computers on a daily basis. Few of the attacksnamely: Denial of Service, Probe, R2L, U2R are very harmful to computer.

With today's technologies, minimizing security breaches is extremely difficult. As a result, intrusion detection has become a significant issue in network security and computer forensics. The major goal is to make the information system run with minimal traffic error.

The process of encoding rules is expensive and lengthy due to the huge amount of network traffic. Using a specificrule-driven language, security personnel can manually alter ordeploynewrules.

Proposed System

Probing, Denial of Service (DoS), Remote to User (R2L), and User to Root (U2R) attacks are just a few of the threats that might harm your system. To detect network breaches, a lot of techniques are used. The Random Forest Algorithm is used to do this. Aim was to use the Train-Test data set to detect network breaches as they happened.

Train-data and Test-data are the two datasets used, each of which comprises fifteen critical attributes for regression. namely: "service," "flag," "src bytes," "dst bytes," "count," "srv count, "serror rate," "same srv rate," "diff srv rate," "dst host diff srv rate," "dst host same src port rate," "dst host srv diff host rate," "dst host serror rate," "dst host srvserror rate," "dst host rerror rate." The Random Forest Classifier (RFC) is applied to the dataset, which is split into training and testing samples.

Random Forest

Random Forests (RF) were first developed by Breiman. RF is a supervised ML algorithm that is mainly used in classification and prediction problems. It uses ensemble techniques such as bagging and boosting. RF is constructed using multiple Decision Trees(DT). Every bootstrapped sample from the initial data has a tree built for it. Each DT will provide its vote on the classification of the object. Figure 1 shows the work flow diagram of the Random Forest. The majority vote is taken as the final classification. The following is how each tree is grown:

In the beginning we consider that there are N data that exist in the original training data. Looking at the original training data, we create a bootstrap sample which takes the size N. This sample will be used to create a fresh training dataset for the tree. Out-of-bag is the data which are present in the training data that was initially built, but is not used in the bootstrap sample (Abebe Tesfahun et al., 2013).

In the original training data, M seems to be the total input features. Only m attributes will be chosen to construct each tree using this bootstrap sample dataset. For each node of the tree, the characteristics from this collection create the best possible split. During the growth of the forest, the value of m should stay unchanged (Tarun Dhar Diwan et al., 2021).

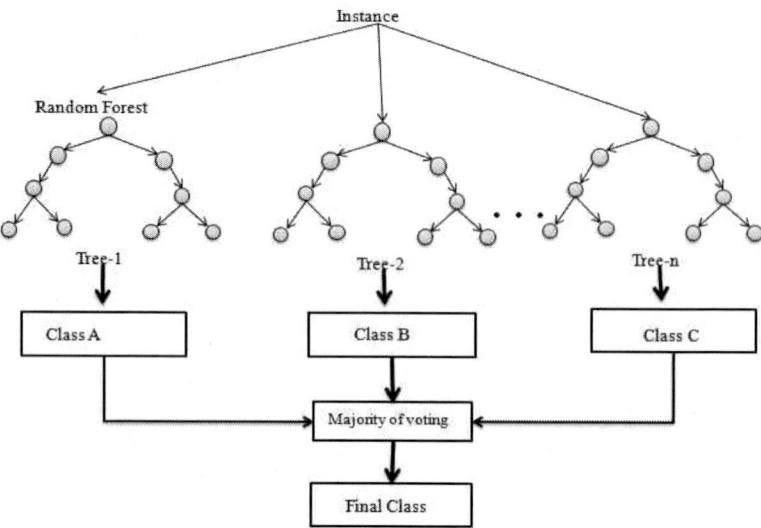

Figure 1. Work flow diagram-RandomForest.

Feature Selection

The Classifier increases the accuracy as well as reduces the data size and improve data comprehension and visualisation. Identifying effective features which have the best ability to discriminate between classes is one of the primary feature limitation concerns. There are two common techniques forminimizing features: Filter and wrapper. Function selection is utilised for Information Gain criterion(IG). Touse Information Gainasa function, each data attribute's entropy value must be calculated (Subburaj et al., 2017) (Subburaj et al., 2019).

In order to determine information gain (IG), entropy prior to and after a transformation is compared. As a result of the application of mutual information, we can calculate the statistical dependence between two variables.

Attack Classification

Experiments with the Train-Test data set are used in the detection of various attacks that can occur in a network Communication (Rahul Vigneswaran et al., 2021). There are namely four types of attacks as follows:

1. *DoS (Distributed Denial of Service):* Itis a type of attackwhere in which the user isdenied access to a perfectly safewebsite. The genuine users are consideredinvalid to enter a website safely.
2. *Remote to User (R2L):* In R2L where in an unidentified person without access to a remote machine transmits packets over a computer networks so that he can exploit that machine and its vulnerability to get access to user's personal computer.
3. *User to Root (U2R):* Here, the hacker will use a normal account of a user to get access to their personal computer andthen exploits confidentiality, trust of the user's system and acts as the administrator of that system.
4. *Probing:* A probing attack occurs when a unidentified person searching a network of computers for information's oral ready present flaws to gain the personal records of the user.

System Architecture

The raw data-set is read into the model where pre-processing and feature selection is carried out. The experimentis carried out on the dataset which are Train.csv and Test.csv. The reason for selecting the csv files uded for the experiment are that the training along with testing datasets in the data-set have a substantial number of redundant number of values in that file. The experiments were carried out on a total of 125973 rows 42 columns. The reason for choosing RandomForest is because it can build multiple decision trees to whichthe random forest and be applied later on, in practice we can conclude that more the trees in the forest the more accurate the prediction will be and hence can achieve higher accuracy. Figure 2 shows the Intrusion detection system architecture.

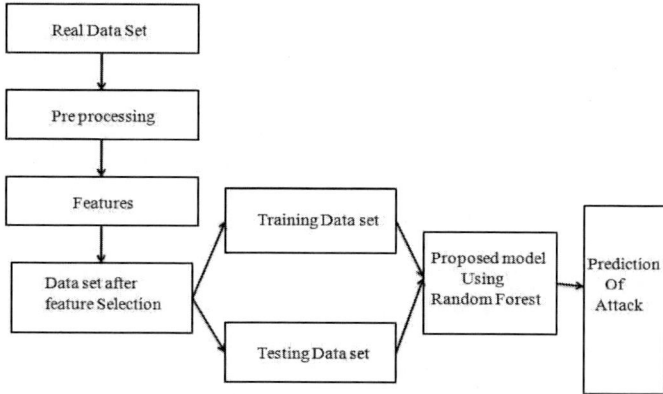

Figure 2. System Architecture for intrusion Detection System.

When the loading of dataset is complete, the first stage is data pre-processing, which involved going the model to see if there are any outliers. Outliers should be removed if they are present. Next, the proposed system is screened for the presence of categorical variables. Extract these categorical data from both test and train data. Later on these categorical data are encoded. Now the target column is separated from these categorical data. The next phase in Intrusion Detection is Feature Selection and Extraction, which is performed out using the RFE (Recursive Feature Elimination) technique. Using this method, only 15 features are determined to represent the assaults category. Following the selection of features using the RFE (Recursive Feature

… Elimination) technique, the next step is to categorise the various types of assaults based on the various characteristics across the network and assess their accuracy, precision, recall, and support.

Methodology

Random Forest

Random Forest has two phases, the very first requirement is to construct the trees taking a sample from the data-set that contains N decision trees, and the second it is required to detect or predict the outcome from each tree and perform the voting method (Subburaj et al., 2017) (Subburaj et al., 2021).

- Step 1: From the training set, choose a bootstrapped dataset.
- Step 2: Constructing decision trees for the sample of data.
    - Choosing m features randomly from p features.
    - Using the best split point and information gain among the m characteristics, determine the noded.
    - $IG(T, A) = ENTROPY(T) - \sum_{V=0}^{n} \epsilon\, A\left(\frac{T_V}{T}\right) . ENTROPY\ (T_V)$

$$\tag{1}$$

    - Splitting nodes in to daughter nodes.
    - Repeating steps I through III until there is a complete DecisionTree.
- Step 3: Repeat Steps 1 and 2 for a Nth time to produce a Nth number of trees.
- Step 4: Note down the output for new data points from each decision tree, and make sure to assign the labels that have the most votes.

Algorithm

Algorithm to predict the intrusions in a networking system

- Input: training dataset D=(x1,y1),(x2,y2)...(xm,ym);

- This contains the actual dataset with malicious target class.
- Output: H(x): The result of the vote from x;
- CRF: Random Forest Classifier where Rfii = 1,2,....,N
- Initialize the sampling size to be null as of now CRF=0
- D` is the new generated sample through feature selection.
- Build multiple decision trees
- **while TRUE do**
- *i*=0
- **for j=1,2,...N do**
- *Dj←Bootstrapsample*
- *Tree$_j$←Decision Tree*
- endfor
- endwhile
- Perform majority voting method for each random trees
- returnH(x)

Here the training data-set is given to the classifier in the beginning that contains x rows and y attributes. X is the potential anomaly data that is present in the train.csv dataset. The Random Forest Classifier will be initialized to null. For every nodes decision tree is constructed and each tree outputsthe classification of object. The majority voting is taken to be the final output (N. Venkateswaran et al., 2020)

Maximum Vote Calculation

$$H(X) = MAX\{C_j, D'jif \sum_{i=1}^{D} h_i^j(x) > 0.5 \sum_{i=1}^{D} \sum_{i=1}^{D} h_i^k(x)\} \qquad (2)$$

Here each Decision Tree will output at the classification of the object and the major classification is considered to be the final output which is done through voting mechanism.

C_j is the result of a set of decision trees and D`j contains the value of other decision trees leaving C_j. The maximum of these two is taken as the outcome of the model.

Network Anomaly Detection Using a Random Forest Classifier

Random Forest vs Other Technologies

- Compared to Decision Trees, Random Forests can provide accurate results without overfitting.
- A logistic regression must have a lower or equal number of noise variables than explanatory variables. The Random forest performance improves with more explanatory variables
- Using ensemble learning, bagging improves Machine Learning accuracy and stability. In contrast, random forest eliminates the complexity of overfitting models and is good in unbalanced and missing data situations.

Result

Table 1. Confusion Matrix

		TrueClass			
Normal	36760	1	0	0	0
DoS	3	53883	0	0	0
Probe	0	2	9312	0	0
R2L	2	8	0	770	0
U2R	0	2	0	0	35

```
  dst_host_srv_rerror_rate xAttack prediction
0                     0.00  normal     normal
1                     0.00  normal      probe
2                     0.00     dos        dos
3                     0.01  normal     normal
4                     0.00  normal     normal
5                     1.00     dos        dos
6                     0.00     dos        dos
7                     0.00     dos        dos
8                     0.00     dos        dos
9                     0.00     dos        dos
```

Figure 3. Represents the predicted classes for the given dataset.

To predict the model's performance, the Confusion Matrix is used which is a Table 1. Each cell of the table represents the correct and incorrect predictions respectively. Here our example contains 5 class classification dataset describing each attacks: Normal, DoS, Probe, R2L, U2R as represented in table. If K = 16 then the mean accuracy of our model is found to be 0.9983627369118869. This indicates the overall accuracy of detecting the intrusions using Random Forest Model is very high. Among the models with k values from 16 to 19, the model with K value 16 holds the highest accuracy of 99%.

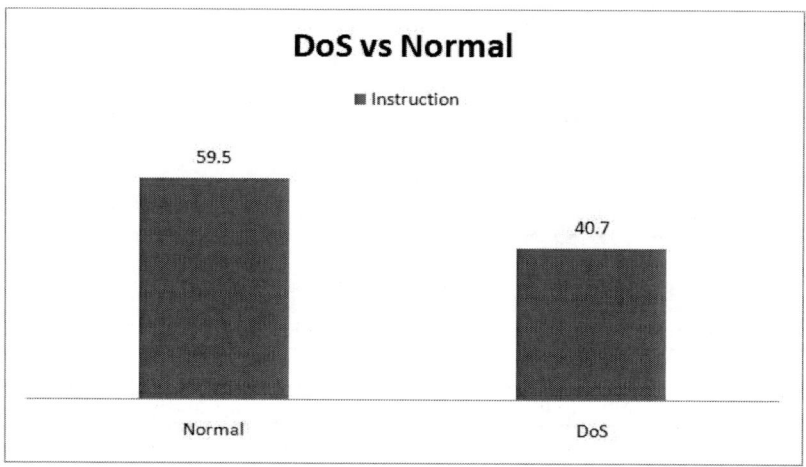

Figure 4. Barchart : Dos vs Normal.

Figure 3 shows the representation of the predicted classes for the given dataset. From the training data set the number of intrusions that occur are counted using value counts () function. The intrusions are classified under the column named "class." There are totally 59.5 percent normal intrusions while 40.7 percent are Denial to service. Figure 4 shows the Bar chart foer comparision of Normal and Denial of Servcie.

Here from the training data set the number of intrusions that occur are counted using value counts () function. The intrusions are classified under the column named "class." There are totally 59.5 percent normal intrusions while 40.7 percent are Probe. Figure 5 shows the Bar chart foer comparision of Normal and Probe.

Here from the training data set the number of intrusion s that occur are counted using value counts () function. The intrusions are classified under the column named "class." There are totally 59.5 percent normal intrusions while 40.7 percent are R2L. Figure 6 shows the Bar chart foer comparision of Normal and R2L.

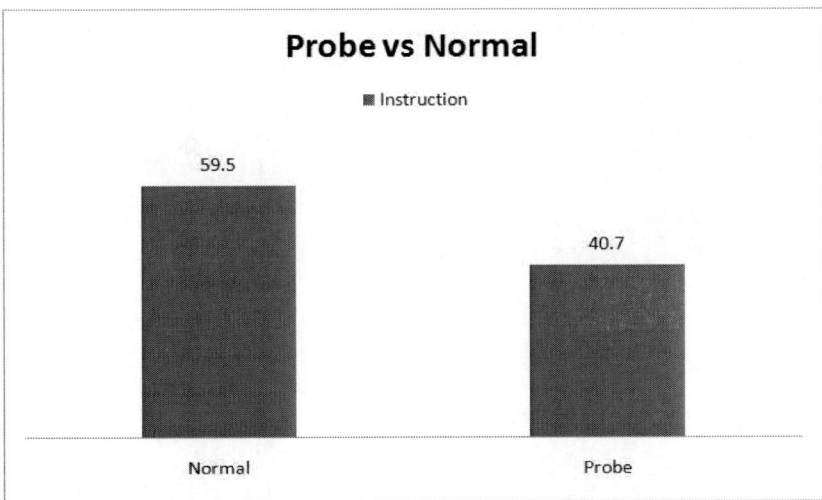

Figure 5. Barchart: Probe vs Normal.

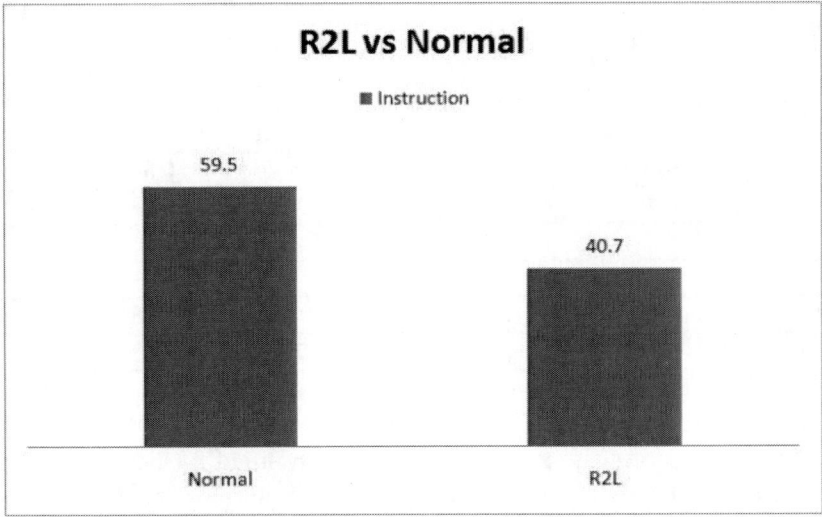

Figure 6. Barchart: R2L vs Normal.

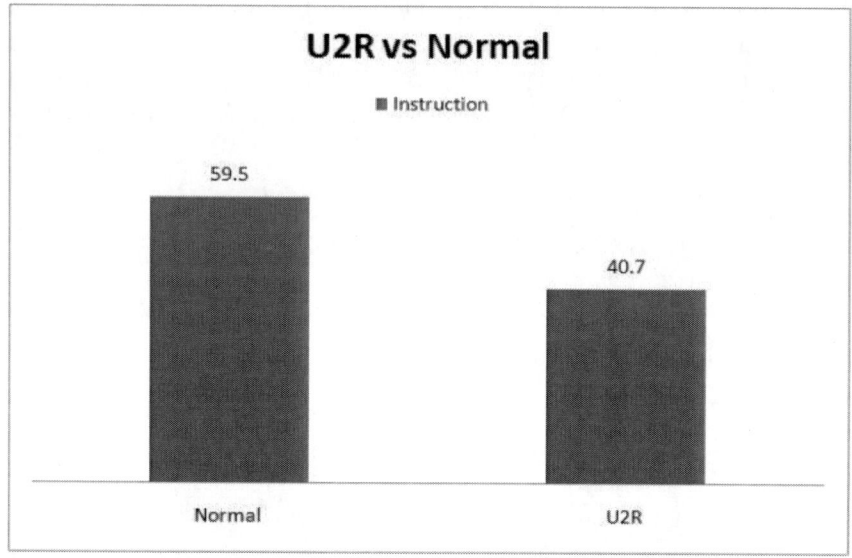

Figure7. Barchart: U2R vs Normal.

Looking at the training dataset the number of intrusions that occur are counted using value counts() function. The intrusions are classified under the column named "class." There are totally 59.5percent normal intrusions while 40.7 percent are U2R. Figure 7 shows the Bar chart foer comparision of Normal and U2R

Table 2. Performance

	Precision	Recall	F1-Score	Support
Normal	1	1	1	53886
DoS	1	1	1	36761
Probe	1	1	1	9314
R2L	1	1	1	780
U2R	1	0.95	0.97	37

Table 2 is a representation of how the model's performance was observed. The table consists of 4 different types that are classified for both actual and predicted cells. The performance table consists of Precision, Recall, F1-Score, Support.

Precision: It gives the percentage of correct predictions were considered to be true.

$$Precision = \frac{True\ Positive}{True\ Positive + FalsePositive} \quad (3)$$

Recall : Using this method, we can determine what percentage of positive samples were correctly predicted as positive by the classifier.

$$Recall = \frac{True Positive}{True\ Positive + False\ Negative} \quad (4)$$

F1-Score: Recall and precision are combined in one measure. In mathematics, it represents precision and recall.

$$F1 - Score = \frac{2 * True Positive}{(2 * True Positive) + False Negative} \quad (5)$$

Support: It appears to imply that the number of instances of each class in the true responses is the support. It can be calculated by adding the rows of the contingency table together (Zeeshan Ahmad et al., 2020).

Conclusion

Modern communication networks include intrusion detection systems asstandard equipment. Toprotect their sensitive data from unauthorised persons, business environments demand a high level of security. This project's dataset was gathered from Kaggle by simulating a wide range of incursions in a military distributed system. For each connection row, 41 features were gathered from both categories. There are two types of class variables: normal and anomalous. The attempted superuser and the number of unsuccessful logins. This offers us a rough notion of how superuser access is linked to failed logins.

Future Work

In future we will propose the anomaly detction based on RF with SDN. In this method we will classify the traffic and identify the atatcks efficiently.

References

Abebe T, Lalitha D. Intrusion Detection using Random Forests Classifier with SMOTE and Feature Reduction. *IEEE International Conference on Cloud Ubiquitous Computing Emerging Technologies*: (2013):128- 132.

Praneet S, Jishnu J, Akhil P and Reshmi M. Edge-Detect: Edge-centric Network Intrusion Detection using Deep Neural Network. *IEEE 18th Annual Consumer Communications & Networking Conference:* (2021): 1-6.

Rahul V, Vinayakumar, Soman K P and Prabaharan P. Evaluating Shallow and Deep Neural Networks for Network Intrusion Detection Systems in Cyber Security. *IEEE - 43488* (2018): 1-6.

Subburaj T and Suthendran K. Threat detection on UDP Protocols using Packet rates in IoT. *Machine Intelligence and smart systems, Springer* (2021): 675 – 682.

Subburaj T and Suthendran K. Detection and Trace back of Low and High Volume of DDoS attack based on Statistical Measures. *Concurrency and Computation: Practice and Experience, Wiley Publications* (2019) : 1-22.

Subburaj T, Suthendran K and Arumugam S. Statistical Approach to Trace the Source of Attack Based on the Variability in Data Flows. *Lecture Notes in Computer Science, LNCS 10398, Springer* (2017): 392-400.

Subburaj T and Suthendran K. Detection and Trace Back of DDoS Attack Based on Statistical Approach. *Journal of Advanced Research in Dynamical and Control Systems 13-Special Issue* (2017): 66-74.

Tarun D D, Siddartha C and Hota H.S. A Detailed Analysis on NSL-KDD Dataset using various Machine Learning Techniques for Intrusion Detection. *Turkish Journal of Computer and Mathematics Education* (2021) 12(11) : 2954-2968.

Venkateswaran N and Umadevi K. Hybridized Wrapper Filter Using Deep Neural Network for Intrusion Detection. *Computer Systems Science & Engineering* (2020) 42(1): 1-14.

Yasir H, Sugumaran M and Journaux L. Machine Learning Techniques for Intrusion Detection: A Comparative Analysis. *Proceedings of the International Conference on Informatics and Analytics Article 53*: (2016): 1-6.

Zeeshan A, Adnan S K, Cheah W S, Johari A and Farhan A. Network intrusion detection system: A systematic study of machine learning and deep learning approaches, *Transactions on Emerging Telecommunications Technologies, Wiley* (2020) 32(1): 1-29.

Chapter 5

A Comprehensible Decision Tree Based on LDA and PCA

Asit Patra
Monalisa Jena[*]
and Satchidananda Dehuri
Department of Computer Science, Fakir Mohan University, Balasore, Odisha, India

Abstract

In this work, an effort has been made to enhance the comprehensibility of the decision tree classifier by employing Principal Component Analysis (PCA) and Linear Discriminant Analysis (LDA). LDA, a supervised method for dimensionality reduction, is used to identify a feature subspace that maximizes the separability between groups while minimizing the within-group separability. On the other hand, PCA, as an unsupervised technique, identifies the direction of maximum variation in the dataset. The dimensions of the datasets are initially reduced separately using LDA and PCA, and subsequently, the decision tree is used for classification in both scenarios. A thorough comparative analysis has been conducted to assess the effectiveness of Classification and Regression Tree (CART), and the decision tree (CART) based on PCA (PCA-DT) and LDA (LDA-DT) by considering a few real-life datasets. Experimental details show that the comprehensibility and performance of the decision tree classifier increase when the datasets are pre-processed using PCA and LDA. Additionally, it has been observed that LDA-DT performs well for datasets with a higher number of attributes, whereas PCA-DT performs well for datasets with relatively fewer attributes.

---

[*] Corresponding Author's Email: bmonalisa.26@gmail.com.

In: Information and Knowledge Systems
Editors: Manaswini Pradhan and Satchidananda Dehurl
ISBN: 979-8-89113-303-7
© 2024 Nova Science Publishers, Inc.

Keywords: machine learning, dimensionality reduction, classification, decision tree, PCA, LDA, prediction

Introduction

Machine learning has become an indispensable part of our daily lives in the modern era and its influence is steadily increasing [1]. Machine learning is widely used in the fields of stock prediction [2], image recognition [3], medical evaluation [4], statistical arbitrage [5], recommendation engines [6], business analysis [7], speech recognition [8], and many more. Classification [9, 10] is one such machine learning technique used for identifying the patterns in existing datasets and predicting discrete values. It is used for categorizing the data points into different classes. In other words, it is the process of developing a model based on training and testing sets and then using it to classify unseen data points provided the model's accuracy is acceptable. Decision tree is a classification technique which resembles a tree structure having root node, internal nodes, branches, and leaf nodes [11]. It is a divide-and-conquer approach to classification that resembles a tree-like structure. Figure 1 showcases a simple instance of a decision tree constructed using the Iris dataset sourced from the UCI repository [12]. The internal nodes represent the conditions determining the branches to be followed to reach the desired leaf node that resembles the desired output.

The decision tree is considered to be among the most powerful classifiers available, as it offers a more visually intuitive representation of the dataset compared to other classification techniques. However, the performance and interpretability of decision tree generally decreases while dealing with huge datasets having large number of attributes. In this chapter, we aim to highlight the advantages of using the feature extraction techniques PCA and LDA to improve the accuracy of traditional classification techniques like decision tree. Feature extraction is used to reduce the dimensions in high-dimensional dataset to a comparatively lower dimension while retaining most of the classification information [13, 14]. Pre-processing the dataset using this technique before applying decision tree can remove the redundant attributes, reduce over-fitting, and reduce the training time. The same is verified through the results of our experiments using PCA [15] and LDA [16]. PCA is one of the popular dimensional reduction approaches to reduce the dimension by maximizing the variance of the features. The lower dimension attributes formed are known as principal components. In contrast, LDA shifts the data to lower dimensions by minimizing inter-class variance and maximizing the between-class variance. Although, both the techniques have their own advantages and disadvantages, there is a trend for selecting LDA over PCA for higher dimensional datasets. This is primarily due to the fact that LDA deals with the variance between the classes, while PCA is absolutely ignorant of the class structures and deals only with the variance of the features. However, if the training set is small, the performance of PCA may outperform LDA [17].

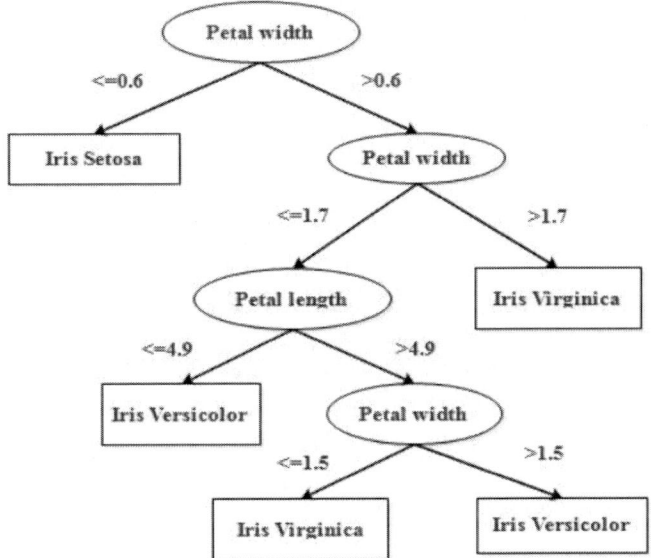

Figure 1. A sample decision tree.

Literature Review

This section highlights several research works related to dimensionality reduction and classification. Belson [18] used the concept of decision tree for biological classification. Swain et al. [19] proposed two methods for designing decision trees using means, covariance matrices, and heuristic search techniques. They used Gaussian maximum likelihood rule as the decision rule and experimented with their models on multi-spectral remote sensing data. Breiman et al. [20] introduced CART algorithm and used the methodology for the classification of spatial patterns of electroencephalography (EEG). Song and Ying [21] gave a comparative view of several DT algorithms along with their applications in several fields. In addition, they described the SPSS and SAS programs to visualize the tree structures. Gavankar [22] proposed a new decision tree technique that could handle the problem of unknown values in testing data in decision tree. He applied his model on PlayTennis data and compared the performance with ID3 technique. Levine [23] discussed several problems and philosophies associated with image processing and highlighted the impact of feature extraction algorithms for pattern recognition. Nevatia and Babu [24] used edge detection and line linking for feature extraction. They highlighted the results by applying their technique on road detection and airport recognition images.

Lee and Landgrebe [25] proposed a feature extraction technique for classification directly based on decision boundaries. They described the relation between decision boundary and the discriminant redundant and informative features. They applied their model on crops dataset in which the results obtained are exceptionally better as compared to existing models. Sun et al. [26] developed a new approach on C4.5 decision tree and PCA to identify the faults in rotating machinery. Their approach achieved better performance with less time for training phase as compared to the backpropagation neural network. Hu et al. [27] employed Principal Component Analysis (PCA) in conjunction with a decision tree to address the challenges of handling large, continuous, and multi-attributed abnormal data. They compared their model with a traditional decision tree based on C4.5 algorithm, and evaluated it on a customer loan database. The experimental analysis revealed that their approach not only improved prediction accuracy, but also resulted in a simplified decision tree model. Zhang et al. [28] proposed a technique with a combination of Wavelet transform; PCA, independent component analysis (ICA) and ID3 based decision tree classification for classifying Electrocardiogram (ECG) signals. They compared the performance of their model with Hermite-SOM, BSS Fourier-SVM, PCA-MLP, DWT-MLP, Morphology-MLP, CWTSVD, Hermit-FNN, and HOS/Hermite-SVM classifiers. The accuracy obtained by their model was 96.31%.

Li et al. [29] combined the CART with PCA algorithm for intrusion detection applications. They applied their model on KDD CUP 1999 dataset and compared the performance with ID3 and C4.5 algorithms. Arowolo et al. [30] used a high dimensional RNA-seq dataset of malaria vectors for their experimental work. To extract latent components from the dataset, they used the PCA algorithm. The extracted components were then classified using kNN and DT classifiers. Their experiments achieved accuracy of 86.7% and 83.3%

for the respective classifiers. Mrva et al. [31] proposed a 3D visualization for effective decision tree exploration and interpretation. They used a combination of random linear combination, PCA, and LDA for extracting informative features from Pima Indians Diabetes dataset and trained the decision tree using DecisionTreeClassifier implementation in scikit-learn package.

Li [32] proposed a decision tree algorithm named SURPASS by combining the concepts of Linear Discriminant with decision tree. He applied his models on several real-world datasets and proved that their model is quite efficient in handling large datasets. He compared the performances with LDA and Rainforest classifiers. Jana et al. [33] proposed a model for predicting the gender and age using facial image data using LDA and subspace ensemble learning techniques. Alajas et al. [34] proposed a technique combining LDA, classification tree (CTree), and regression tree (RTree) for classification. They compared the performance of their model to several techniques CSVM, RSVM, GPR, NB, and KNN and found the accuracy of 97.79% and R^2 of 0.943.

Background Details

This section represents the essential methodologies related to our chapter.

Decision Tree

The decision tree algorithm adheres to the divide and conquer paradigm, making it applicable for both classification and regression tasks [35]. It can be depicted as a tree-like structure with a designated root node at the top. The root is selected using attribute selection measures. The leaf nodes represent the final outcomes, branches represent the decision rules and the internal nodes represent the attributes or features of the dataset. One of the principal benefits of DT is that it provides easy interpretation of the data. It can be used to visually represent the decisions and their makings.

Different Splitting Criteria Used for Decision Tree Construction
Splitting criteria defines the basis on which the parent nodes are further split into their child nodes. Numerous splitting criteria have been used in recent times [36], some of which are mentioned below:

1. *Entropy:* Entropy is a measure of uncertainty. It is calculated using the formula:

$$Entropy(D) = \sum_{i=1}^{c} -p_i \log_2(pi) \qquad (1)$$

where *pi* defines the non-zero probability that a tuple in D belongs to the class C.

2. *Information Gain:* It is defined as the amount of information provided by an attribute about a class. It is calculated using the formula:

$$Gain(D, A) = Entropy(D) - \sum_{j=1}^{v} \frac{|D_j|}{|D|} Entropy(D_j) \qquad (2)$$

where, *D* defines a given data partition, *A* represents an attribute and *D* is split into *v* partitions.

3. *Gain Ratio:* It is an extension of information gain that utilizes the splitting criteria for its calculation. The formula for splitting information has been defined below:

$$SplitInfoA = -\sum_{j=1}^{v} \frac{|D_j|}{|D|} \log_2 \left(\frac{|D_j|}{|D|}\right) \qquad (3)$$

Gain ratio can be calculated using:

$$GainRatio(A) = \frac{Gain(A)}{SplitInfoA(D)} \qquad (4)$$

4. *Gini Index:* Gini index aims to reduce the impurities. It is calculated using the formula :

$$Gini(D) = 1 - \sum_{i=1}^{m} p_i^2 \qquad (5)$$

Steps for Building a Decision Tree
Here the steps for building a decision tree are represented. It uses information gain as the splitting criteria. Table 1 represents the *Play Golf* dataset from the kaggle repository that describes various factors deciding whether a person should go out to play golf or not.

Table 1. A Sample Dataset

Outlook	Temp.	Humidity	Windy	PlayGolf
R	H	Hi	F	N
R	H	Hi	T	N
O	H	Hi	F	Y
S	M	Hi	F	Y
S	C	N	F	Y
S	C	N	T	N
O	C	N	T	Y
R	M	Hi	F	N
R	C	N	F	Y
S	M	N	F	Y
R	M	N	T	Y
O	M	Hi	T	Y
O	H	N	F	Y
S	M	Hi	T	N

Description: R:Rainy, O:Overcast, S:Sunny; H:Hot, C:Cool, M:Mild; Hi:High, N:Normal; T:True, F:False; Y:Yes, N:No.

Step 1: Determining the decision attribute

The first step is to determine the decision attribute and find out the classes which form the basis for classification. In our example, we have the decision attribute named as *Play Golf* and we have two classes: Yes and No.

Step 2: Constructing the frequency table

Table 2 displays a frequency distribution, indicating the number of elements in each class.

Table 2. Class Frequency

Play Golf (14)	
Y	N
9	5

Step 3: Calculating the entropy of the decision attribute

Let the number of elements in the *Yes* and *No* classes be represented as Y and N, respectively. The entropy of the attribute *Play Golf* can be calculated as:

$$E\,(PlayGolf) = -\left(\frac{Y}{Y+N}\log_2\frac{Y}{Y+N}\right) - \left(\frac{N}{Y+N}\log_2\frac{N}{Y+N}\right)$$
$$= -\left(\frac{9}{14}\log_2\frac{9}{14}\right) - \left(\frac{5}{14}\log_2\frac{5}{14}\right) \qquad (6)$$
$$= -(0.357\log_2 0.357) - (0.643\log_2 0.643) = 0.94$$

Step 4: Computing the entropy of the remaining attributes in relation to the decision attribute

To begin, we will compute the entropy of the *Outlook* attribute in relation to the *Play Golf* attribute, denoted as *E (PlayGolf, Outlook)*. The frequency table for the *Outlook* attribute can be constructed as shown in Table 3.

1. The *Outlook* attribute contains three attribute values *Sunny (S)*, *Overcast (O)*, and *Rainy (R)*.

Table 3. Class Frequency for *Outlook*

		Play Golf(14)		
		Yes	No	Total
Outlook	S	3	2	5
	O	4	0	4
	R	2	3	5

The entropy for each value can be calculated as:

$$E\,(S) = -\left(\frac{3}{5}\log_2\frac{2}{5}\right) - \left(\frac{3}{5}\log_2\frac{2}{5}\right)$$
$$= -(0.6\log_2 0.6) - (0.4\log_2 0.4) \qquad (7)$$
$$= 0.971$$

Similarly, entropy obtained for other attribute values are:

$E(O) = 0$ (8)

$E(R) = 0.971$ (9)

Now, the entropy of *Outlook* attribute with respect to *Play Golf* can be calculated as:

$$E(PlayGolf, Outlook)$$
$$= \frac{Y(S)}{Y+N}E(S) + \frac{Y(O)}{Y+N}E(O) + \frac{Y(R)}{Y+N}E(R)$$
$$= \frac{5}{14}0.971 + \frac{4}{14}0 + \frac{5}{14}0.971 = 0.693 \quad (10)$$

Similarly, we can calculate the entropy of all the attributes as follows:

$$E(PlayGolf, Temperature) = 0.911 \quad (11)$$

$$E(PlayGolf, Humidity) = 0.788 \quad (12)$$

$$E(PlayGolf, Windy) = 0.892 \quad (13)$$

Step 5: Measure the information gain
It can be computed as:

$$Gain\,(S,T) = Entropy\,(S) Entropy\,(S,T) \quad (14)$$

where S represents the decision attribute, and T represents all other attributes.

$$Gain\,(PlayGolf, Outlook) = E(\,PlayGolf) - E(PlayGolf, Outlook)$$
$$= 0.94 - 0.693 = 0.247 \quad (15)$$
$$Gain\,(PlayGolf, Temperature)$$
$$= E(PlayGolf) - E(PlayGolf, Temperature) \quad (16)$$
$$= 0.029$$

$$Gain\,(PlayGolf, Humidity) = E(PlayGolf) - E(PlayGolf, Humidity)$$
$$= 0.152 \quad (17)$$

$$Gain\,(PlayGolf, Windy)$$
$$= E(PlayGolf)$$
$$- E(PlayGolf, Windy)$$
$$= 0.048 \quad (18)$$

Step 6: Performing the split

The *Outlook* attribute, is selected to serve as the root node as it has the highest information gain value, and subsequently, the tree is constructed. The tree formed has been represented in Figure 2. In this step, we obtained only one leaf node under *Overcast* value of *Outlook*. Hence, our tree needs to be split further under *Sunny* and *Rainy* attribute values till all the leaf nodes are obtained.

Step 7: Constructing the final tree

Now, the table can be split into three parts based on the *Outlook* attribute (root node) as shown in Table 4. The splitting continues till all the leaf nodes are discovered by evaluating each part individually using steps 1 to 7. The fully constructed tree is shown in Figure 3.

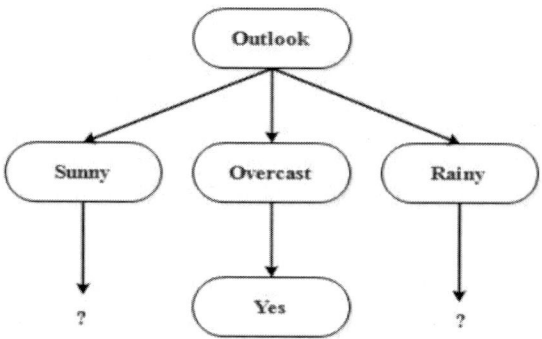

Figure 2. Decision Tree with *outlook* attribute as the root node.

Advantages of Decision Tree

1. Decision tree falls under the category of predictive modeling and can be utilized for both classification and regression tasks. In classification, decision tree predicts discrete values or class labels, while in regression; it predicts continuous values.
2. Decision tree provides a graphical representation of the data, which makes it highly interpretable.
3. Decision trees do not require data normalization as a pre-processing step when used for classification.
4. Decision trees are non-parametric models that can effectively handle non-linear datasets.

Disadvantages of Decision Tree

1. Decision trees require more time and memory for handling numerical data.
2. Decision tree may suffer from over-fitting issues if proper techniques are not used.
3. Decision trees are not quite reusable as a minor updates may require the construction of a completely different tree structure.

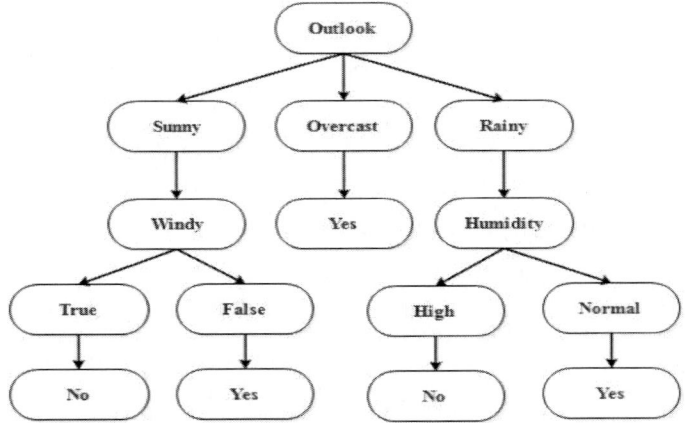

Figure 3. Fully Constructed Decision tree.

Table 4. Dataset split according to *Outlook* attribute

Outlook	Temp.	Humidity	Windy	PlayGolf
S	M	Hi	F	Y
S	C	N	F	Y
S	C	N	T	N
S	M	N	F	Y
S	M	Hi	T	N
O	H	Hi	F	Y
O	C	N	T	Y
O	M	Hi	T	Y
O	H	N	F	Y
R	H	Hi	F	N
R	H	Hi	T	N
R	M	Hi	F	N
R	C	N	F	Y
R	M	N	T	Y

Applications of Decision Tree

Decision trees have several applications in various fields. Some of them are mentioned below:

1. Decision trees are highly effective in solving bio-informative problems. They are used in annotating multilevel genomics sequences, finding genes in DNA sequences and predicting operon structures in the genomics sequences of prokaryotes.
2. Decision trees have been widely used in healthcare for classifying different types of diseases.
3. Decision trees are used for analyzing customer behaviours, formulating business decisions and strategies.
4. Decision trees are also used for classification and prediction of biological activity from chemical structure of drugs.
5. In banking, decision trees are widely used for evaluating a customer's creditworthiness before providing loans to prevent losses.

Principal Component Analysis

PCA is a dimensionality reduction method used for reducing the number of attributes of large datasets along with retaining most of the discriminant information [37]. The PCA algorithm is used to map the important information from the dataset into new set of attributes. These are called as principal components. However, this step is not reversible as some information is lost while reducing the dimension (number of attributes).

PCA generally tries to project the higher-dimensional data to a lower-dimension by evaluating the variance of each attribute because attributes having higher variance results in better split between the classes. PCA is known to enhance the visualization of datasets by reducing the number of attributes, leading to a more concise representation of the data that is easier to visualize and interpret.

Working Principle of PCA

The functioning of a PCA algorithm can be elucidated in the following sequence:

1. *Standardization of the dataset:* PCA is quite sensitive to the variance of the features. As a result, the features with larger ranges will dominate over the features with smaller ranges and this will lead to a biased result. Therefore, standardization is performed so that each feature can contribute equally for the result calculations. This is done using the formula:

$$X_{new} = \frac{X - \mu}{\sigma} \tag{19}$$

where X refers to the original dataset, μ and σ are the mean and standard deviations of their respective features, respectively.

2. *Calculation of the covariance matrix:* Let the dataset consists of m features. The covariance matrix (γ) can be calculated as follows:

$$\gamma(x, y) = \frac{\sum (x_i - \bar{x}) * (y_i - \bar{y})}{N} \tag{20}$$

$$\sigma^2(x) = \gamma(x, x) = \frac{\sum (x_i - \bar{x})^2}{N} \tag{21}$$

Here, N and σ^2 are the total number of elements in the respective features, and variance, respectively. The detailed calculation is shown in Table 5.

Table 5. Calculation of covariance matrix

	f1	f2	f3	...	fn
f1	σ^2(f1)	γ(f1,f2)	γ(f1,f3)	...	γ(f1,fn)
f2	γ(f2,f1)	σ^2(f2)	γ(f2,f3)	...	γ(f2,fn)
f3	γ(f3,f1)	γ(f3,f2)	σ^2(f3)	...	γ(f3,fn)
.	.	.	.	.	.
.	.	.	.	.	.
.	.	.	.	.	.
fn	γ(fn,f1)	γ(fn,f2)	γ(fn,f3)	...	σ^2(fn)

3. *Calculation of Eigen values and Eigen vectors:* After computing the covariance matrix, the subsequent step involves determining the eigenvalues and eigenvectors of the matrix. The eigenvalues can be calculated using the following formula:

$$\det(\gamma - \lambda I) = 0 \tag{22}$$

Here, *det* denotes the determinant of the matrix $\gamma - \lambda I$. Eigen values are obtained as a result of solving for λ in an equation. Eigen vectors are obtained by solving the following equation for v vector with different Eigen values (λ) using the Cramer's rule:

$$(\gamma - \lambda I)v = 0 \tag{23}$$

4. *The Eigen values (λ) and Eigen vectors (v)* are sorted in a non-increasing order.
5. *Then top k Eigen values* are chosen and their corresponding Eigen vectors are used to form a matrix of selected Eigen vectors (F_S).
6. *The transformed data matrix* is created by multiplying the standardized feature matrix with the selected Eigen vector matrix.

$$\textit{Transformed data matrix} = X_{new} * F_S \tag{24}$$

Limitations of PCA

While PCA is a commonly used method for addressing dimensionality reduction challenges, it is not without its limitations. Some of these are outlined below:

- Some discriminant information may be lost when the dimensionality is reduced via PCA. The classification performance may be affected as a result.
- PCA relies on linear model and may not perform well while reducing the dimensionality of non-linear datasets. This problem can be solved by shifting the non-linear datasets to a higher dimension to make it linear and then applying PCA for dimensionality reduction.
- The dataset needs to be standardized before applying PCA as the attributes having higher ranges may dominate over the attributes with lower ranges and result in biased outputs.
- PCA transforms the initial features into principal components that may be more difficult to interpret and comprehend compared to the original features.
- PCA may find it difficult to handle datasets with missing data and outliers. Additional techniques are needed to impute missing values.

Linear Discriminant Analysis

LDA is another learning technique for reducing the dimensionality of large datasets to improve readability and reduce the training time [38] [39]. LDA techniques are broadly categorized into two types: class-dependent and class-independent. If the distinct transformation matrices are calculated for each class, resulting in separate lower-dimensional representations for each class then the approach is known as class-dependent. However, if a common transformation matrix is calculated and only one lower dimension is proposed for all the classes then the technique is known as class-independent LDA.

Working of LDA

Let ω_i represent the elements of the classes i to m. The working of a class independent LDA algorithm can be explained through the following steps:

1. Initially, the mean of each class (denoted by μ_j) followed by the total mean of all the classes (denoted by μ) are computed.

2. Then the between-class variance ($SBetween_i$) is computed for each class as follows:

$$SBetween_i = n_i(\mu_i - \mu_i)^T(\mu_i - \mu_i) \tag{25}$$

where n_i, μ_i refers to the number of items and mean of each class, respectively. Here μ refers to the total mean of all the classes.

3. The total between-class variance is obtained by summing the between-class variances of each individual class:

$$SBetween = \sum_{i=0}^{m} SBetween_i \tag{26}$$

4. The next step involves mean centering the data using the formula:

$$d_i = \omega_i - \mu_i \tag{27}$$

where d_i refers to the mean centered data for each class ω_i.

5. Next, the total within-class variance is computed in the following manner:

$$SWithin_i = d_i^T \times d_i \qquad (28)$$

$$SWithin = \sum_{i=0}^{m} SWithin_i \qquad (29)$$

where, $SWithin_i$ denotes the within-class matrix specific to a particular class, whereas $SWithin$ refers to the cumulative within-class matrix for all the classes.

6. The transformation matrix is calculated as:

$$W = SWithin^{-1} \times SBetween \qquad (30)$$

7. The next step involves the calculation of eigenvalues and eigenvectors on the transformation matrix (W).
8. The eigenvalues and their respective vectors are arranged in a descending order based on their values. Then k top eigenvalues are selected (where $k <= m$) and their corresponding eigenvectors picked and placed in a separate matrix (V_S).
9. Subsequently the original data is transformed into a lower-dimensional space (k) using the given formula:

$$Y_i = \omega_i \times V_S \qquad (31)$$

where, Y_i represents the data of ith sample after projection on k-dimension space.

Similarly, the working procedure of a class dependent LDA are summarized as follows:

1. Initially, the overall mean and mean of each class are computed.
2. The Between-class matrix is calculated using equations 25 & 26.
3. The next step is mean centering the data using equation 27.
4. The within-class variance matrix is calculated for each class using equation 28.
5. The transformation matrices for each class is computed as follows :

$$W_i = SWithin_i^{-1} \times SBetween \qquad (32)$$

6. The eigenvalues ($\lambda_{\omega i}$) and eigenvectors ($V_{\omega i}$) are calculated for each transformation matrix (W_i) separately.

7. For transforming the dataset into a lower k-dimension space, for each class, the best k eigenvalues are selected and their corresponding eigenvectors picked and placed in a separate matrix (V_{Si}).
8. Now, the original data is transformed into a lower-dimensional space (k) using the formula:

$$Y_i = \omega_i \times V_{Si} \qquad (33)$$

where, Y_i represents the ith sample data after being projected onto the k-dimensional space.

Both the LDA methods can be used for transforming the data from a higher dimension space to a lower dimension space. However, class-independent method is mostly used rather than class-dependent method as it involves less CPU calculations and computation time.

Limitations of LDA

While LDA is a versatile technique, it may encounter certain limitations. Some of them are discussed below:

1. One of the limitations of LDA is small sample size (SSS) problem, wherein the number of dimensions exceeds the number of data points present in the matrix. It results in the singularity of the within-class variance matrix (SWithin). There are many techniques proposed to solve the SSS problems. Some of them are discussed below:
   - *Regularization:* To ensure that the within-class matrix is non-singular, a scaled identity matrix is added to it. It can be represented as *SWithin*= *SWithin*+ $\delta \times I$ where, δ is the regularization parameter ($\delta > 0$) that needs to be chosen carefully.
   - *Sub-space:* To enable the within-class matrix to become invertible, this method reduces the dimensionality of the original data to a non-singular intermediate subspace before applying LDA. Typically, PCA is employed at the outset for dimensionality reduction. So, this technique is also known as PCA+LDA technique. However, the performance may be degraded as PCA may neglect some discriminant information.
   - *Null-space:* To ensure the non-singularity of the within-class variance matrix, the process involves removing its null space. Generally, PCA is used to find the optimal vectors. However,

removal of null space results in degradation of the performance as much discriminant information is lost.
2. Apart from these, several other techniques can be used to solve the SSS problems like Orthogonal LDA (OLDA), QRNLDA, Fast NLDA, Pseudo-inverse LDA, Exploration LDA, Maximum uncertainty LDA, Two-stage LDA, and many more.
3. LDA may exhibit reduced effectiveness when handling datasets with non-linearly separable classes, as the parameters of LDA are optimized based on the class means. Therefore, if the discriminatory information is not closely tied to the class means, LDA performance may degrade. To mitigate this, one possible solution is to achieve linear separability by mapping the original data into comparatively higher-dimensional space, and subsequently applying LDA to identify a lower-dimensional space where the data can be effectively separated.

Numerical Evaluation

The comparative analysis of traditional decision tree based on CART algorithm, PCA embedded CART for classification (PCA-DT), and LDA embedded CART for classification (LDA-DT) is presented in this section.

Environment Setup
The experiments are performed on a 64-bit Windows operating system with an 11th generation Intel Core i5 processor and a 512 GB SSD. Python (version 3.9.4) is utilized to conduct the experiments, and the Jupyter Notebook IDE is employed.

Dataset Details
For our experimental work, we have considered three datasets derived from the keel repository [40].

- *Movement libras*: LIBRAS comprises of 15 hand movement types, with each type having 24 instances in the dataset.
- *Spectfheart*: The task involves classifying a patient into one of two categories, namely normal (0) or abnormal (1), by analyzing cardiac SPECT images.

- *Satimage*: The dataset comprises of set of satellite images along with class label of sentral pixel values. The classification of the pixels is determined based on their multi-spectral values, and each pixel's class is denoted by a numerical code in this dataset.

All the datasets are composed of numerical data and are appropriate for classification tasks. For more details, Table 6 may be referred.

Table 6. Dataset Details

Sl. No.	Datasets	No. of attributes	No. of tuples	No. of classes
1	movement libras	90	360	15
2	spectfheart	44	267	2
3	satimage	36	6435	7

Results and Discussion

A decision tree can be constructed using several DT induction algorithms. In this work, we have used CART algorithm of DT for classification. Initially we classifiedthe datasets, as mentioned in Table 6, using DT without pre-processing them and we observed the classification accuracy. Then we pre-processed the datasets using PCA and LDA and classified the datasets using DT. In all the cases we have used CART algorithm of DT. It was observed that the performance of the traditional DT is improved effectively by embedding it with dimensionality reduction algorithms LDA and PCA. It is observed that in the first two cases (movement libras and spectfheart), the performance of LDA-DT was better than the PCA-DT. However, in the third case (satimage), PCA-DT outperforms LDA-DT. Table 7 highlights the performance results obtained by applying DT, PCA-DT, and LDA-DT in terms of accuracy, precision, F-measure, and recall. Based on the aforementioned observations, it can be inferred that LDA tends to perform more effectively when the dataset contains a large number of attributes. Conversely, if the dataset has only a limited number of attributes, PCA may outperform LDA. Figure 4-7 provide graphical representations of performance results of various classification approaches.

Table 7. Performance results of the classifiers

DATASET	DT				PCA-DT				LDA-DT			
	Accuracy	Precision	Recall	F-Measure	Accuracy	Precision	Recall	F-Measure	Accuracy	Precision	Recall	F-Measure
Movement libras	0.5833	0.6128	0.5434	0.576	0.7222	0.7548	0.6787	0.7147	0.7962	0.8365	0.7543	0.793
Spectfheart	0.6543	0.7225	0.6212	0.668	0.7901	0.7835	0.7543	0.7686	0.8765	0.8849	0.8545	0.8694
Satimage	0.843	0.848	0.754	0.798	0.8767	0.8757	0.8021	0.8372	0.8493	0.85	0.8324	0.8411

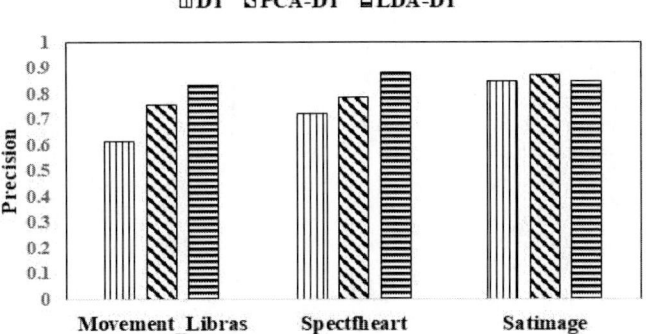

Figure 4. Comparative analysis of DT, PCA-DT, and LDA-DT based on accuracy.

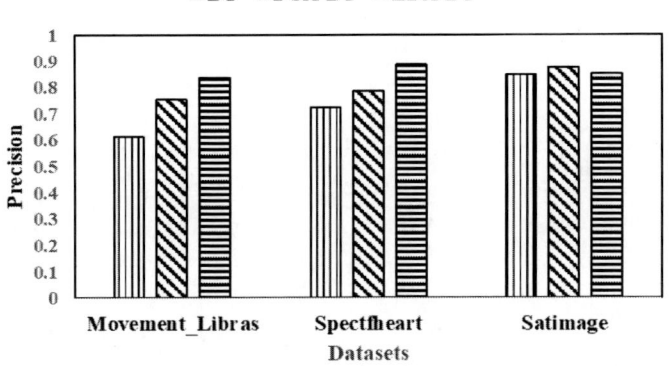

Figure 5. Comparative analysis of DT, PCA-DT, and LDA-DT based on precision.

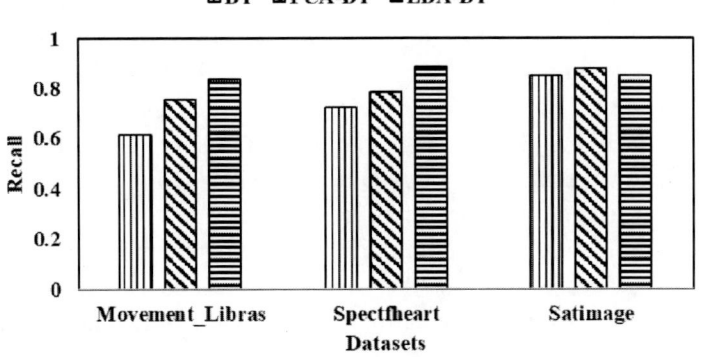

Figure 6. Comparative analysis of DT, PCA-DT, and LDA-DT based on recall.

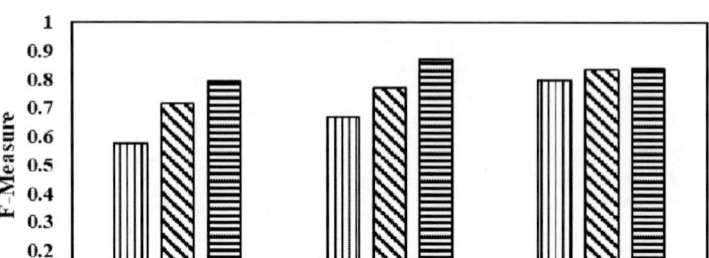

Figure 7. Comparative analysis of DT, PCA-DT, and LDA-DT based on F-measure.

Future Work

The limitations of LDA and the further improvement of LDA-DT will be the primary focus of future work. To overcome challenges such as small sample size problems and null space problems, alternative LDA algorithms, including Direct LDA, PCA+LDA, Null LDA, and Regularization LDA, will be explored. These algorithms offer promising possibilities for addressing the limitations and enhancing the performance of LDA-DT. In addition, the future research will investigate techniques specifically tailored to handle datasets with fewer samples. This will involve developing strategies that can effectively extract meaningful patterns and ensure reliable classification results even when the available samples are limited. Furthermore, strategies for managing high-dimensional datasets will be explored to overcome the complexities associated with the increasing number of attributes. The ultimate goal is to enhance the applicability and effectiveness of LDA-DT in real-world classification tasks. By addressing the limitations of LDA and further optimizing the performance of LDA-DT, the research aims to provide more reliable and accurate solutions for practical use. The advancements made through this future work will contribute to the development of robust and efficient classification algorithms that can be successfully applied in various domains, thereby benefiting decision-making processes and improving overall performance.

Conclusion

In this work, an assessment of the performance of DT, PCA-DT, and LDA-DT was conducted for classification tasks involving datasets with a large number of attributes. The effectiveness of these techniques in handling high-dimensional datasets was evaluated. The impact of feature extraction techniques on the performance of decision trees was explored through rigorous experimentation. Our findings demonstrated that the performance of the traditional decision tree can be significantly enhanced by employing feature extraction techniques during the pre-processing phase. Specifically, when comparing the performance of different feature extraction techniques, we observed that LDA-DT outperformed PCA-DT in scenarios where the datasets consisted of a higher number of attributes. However, it is noteworthy that when the number of attributes was relatively lower, PCA-DT exhibited better performance. This disparity arises from the inherent nature of LDA, which analyzes class structures, and PCA, which primarily considers the variance of the features while disregarding the class labels.

Additionally, our experiments revealed that decision trees integrated with feature extraction techniques exhibited impressive processing times, especially when dealing with larger dimensional datasets. Regardless of the dataset size, the results were generated in less than half a second of processing time on an i5, 11th generation computer. However, it is essential to recognize that while LDA-DT may appear more efficient in managing high-dimensional datasets, the underlying LDA algorithm itself has certain limitations, such as small sample size problems and null space problems. These limitations can be taken into account in future research to ensure a comprehensive understanding and further improvements in the performance of LDA-DT.

References

[1] Nayak, Arpita, and Kaustubh Dutta. "Impacts of machine learning and artificial intelligence on mankind." In *2017 international conference on intelligent computing and control (I2C2)*, pp. 1-3. IEEE, 2017.

[2] Rajendran, Periyasamy, and Muthusamy Madheswaran. "Hybrid medical image classification using association rule mining with decision tree algorithm." *arXiv preprint arXiv:1001.3503* (2010).

[3] Jena, Monalisa, Ranjan Kumar Behera, and Santanu Kumar Rath. "Machine learning models for stock prediction using real-time streaming data." In *Biologically Inspired Techniques in Many-Criteria Decision Making: International Conference*

on *Biologically Inspired Techniques in Many-Criteria Decision Making (BITMDM-2019)*, pp. 101-108. Springer International Publishing, 2020.

[4] Vlahou, Antonia, John O. Schorge, Betsy W. Gregory, and Robert L. Coleman. "Diagnosis of ovarian cancer using decision tree classification of mass spectral data." *Journal of Biomedicine and Biotechnology* 2003, no. 5 (2003): 308-314.

[5] Fischer, Thomas Günter, Christopher Krauss, and Alexander Deinert. "Statistical arbitrage in cryptocurrency markets." *Journal of Risk and Financial Management* 12, no. 1 (2019): 31.

[6] Jadhav, S. D., & Channe, H. P. (2016). Efficient recommendation system using decision tree classifier and collaborative filtering. *Int. Res. J. Eng. Technol*, 3(8), 2113-2118.

[7] Yeo, Benjamin, and Delvin Grant. "Predicting service industry performance using decision tree analysis." *International Journal of Information Management* 38, no. 1 (2018): 288-300.

[8] Shinozaki, Takahiro, and SadaokiFurui. "Error analysis using decision trees in spontaneous presentation speech recognition." In *IEEE Workshop on Automatic Speech Recognition and Understanding, 2001. ASRU'01.*, pp. 198-201. IEEE, 2001.

[9] Kotsiantis, Sotiris B., Ioannis D. Zaharakis, and Panayiotis E. Pintelas. "Machine learning: a review of classification and combining techniques." *Artificial Intelligence Review* 26, no. 3 (2006): 159-190.

[10] Soofi, Aized Amin, and Arshad Awan. "Classification techniques in machine learning: applications and issues." *J. Basic Appl. Sci* 13 (2017): 459-465.

[11] Jena, Monalisa, and Satchidananda Dehuri. "DecisionTree for Classification and Regression: A State-of-the Art Review." *Informatica* 44, no. 4 (2020).

[12] Dua, Dheeru, and Casey Graff. "UCI machine learning repository, 2017." *URL http://archive. ics. uci. edu/ml* 7, no. 1 (2017).

[13] Khalid, Samina, Tehmina Khalil, and Shamila Nasreen. "A survey of feature selection and feature extraction techniques in machine learning." In *2014 science and information conference*, pp. 372-378. IEEE, 2014.

[14] Jena, Monalisa, and Satchidananda Dehuri. "Entropy Based Bayes' Rule for Coping Dimensionality Reduction in Predictive Task of Data Mining." In *2019 Second International Conference on Advanced Computational and Communication Paradigms (ICACCP)*, pp. 1-6. IEEE, 2019.

[15] Smith, Lindsay I. "A tutorial on principal components analysis." (2002).

[16] Tharwat, Alaa, Tarek Gaber, Abdelhameed Ibrahim, and Aboul Ella Hassanien. "Linear discriminant analysis: A detailed tutorial." *AI communications* 30, no. 2 (2017): 169-190.

[17] Martinez, Aleix M., and Avinash C. Kak. "Pca versus lda." *IEEE transactions on pattern analysis and machine intelligence* 23, no. 2 (2001): 228-233.

[18] Belson, William A. "Matching and prediction on the principle of biological classification." *Journal of the Royal Statistical Society: Series C (Applied Statistics)* 8, no. 2 (1959): 65-75.

[19] Swain, Philip H., and Hans Hauska. "The decision tree classifier: Design and potential." *IEEE Transactions on Geoscience Electronics* 15, no. 3 (1977): 142-147.

[20] Grajski, Kamil A., Leo Breiman, Gonzalo Viana Di Prisco, and Walter J. Freeman. "Classification of EEG spatial patterns with a tree-structured methodology: CART." *IEEE transactions on biomedical engineering* 12 (1986): 1076-1086.

[21] Song, Yan-Yan, and L. U. Ying. "Decision tree methods: applications for classification and prediction." *Shanghai archives of psychiatry* 27, no. 2 (2015): 130.

[22] Gavankar, Sachin S., and Sudhirkumar D. Sawarkar. "Eager decision tree." In *2017 2nd International Conference for Convergence in Technology (I2CT)*, pp. 837-840. IEEE, 2017.

[23] Levine, Martin D. "Feature extraction: A survey." *Proceedings of the IEEE* 57, no. 8 (1969): 1391-1407.

[24] Nevatia, Ramakant, and K. Ramesh Babu. "Linear feature extraction and description." *Computer Graphics and Image Processing* 13, no. 3 (1980): 257-269.

[25] Lee, Chulhee, and David A. Landgrebe. "Feature extraction based on decision boundaries." *IEEE Transactions on Pattern Analysis and Machine Intelligence* 15, no. 4 (1993): 388-400.

[26] Sun, Weixiang, Jin Chen, and Jiaqing Li. "Decision tree and PCA-based fault diagnosis of rotating machinery." *Mechanical systems and signal processing* 21, no. 3 (2007): 1300-1317.

[27] Hu, Juanli, Jiabin Deng, and Mingxiang Sui. "A new approach for decision tree based on principal component analysis." In *2009 International Conference on Computational Intelligence and Software Engineering*, pp. 1-4. IEEE, 2009.

[28] Zhang, Leigang, Hu Peng, and Chenglong Yu. "An approach for ECG classification based on wavelet feature extraction and decision tree." In *2010 international conference on wireless communications & signal processing (WCSP)*, pp. 1-4. IEEE, 2010.

[29] Li, Miao. "Application of CART decision tree combined with PCA algorithm in intrusion detection." In *2017 8th IEEE international conference on software engineering and service science (ICSESS)*, pp. 38-41. IEEE, 2017.

[30] Arowolo, MichealOlaolu, Marion Adebiyi, Ayodele Adebiyi, and Olatunji Okesola. "PCA model for RNA-Seq malaria vector data classification using KNN and decision tree algorithm." In *2020 international conference in mathematics, computer engineering and computer science (ICMCECS)*, pp. 1-8. IEEE, 2020.

[31] Mrva, Jakub, ŠtefanNeupauer, LukášHudec, Jakub Ševcech, and Peter Kapec. "Decision support in medical data using 3D decision tree visualisation." In *2019 E-Health and Bioengineering Conference (EHB)*, pp. 1-4. IEEE, 2019.

[32] Li, Xiao-Bai. "A scalable decision tree system and its application in pattern recognition and intrusion detection." *Decision Support Systems* 41, no. 1 (2005): 112-130.

[33] Jana, S., S. Thangam, and S. Selvaganesan. "Gender Identification Using Ensemble Linear Discriminant Analysis Algorithm Based on Facial Features." In *Machine Learning and Autonomous Systems: Proceedings of ICMLAS 2021*, pp. 23-35. Singapore: Springer Nature Singapore, 2022.

[34] Alajas, Oliver John, Ronnie Concepcion, Elmer Dadios, Edwin Sybingco, Christan Hail Mendigoria, and Heinrick Aquino. "Prediction of Grape Leaf Black Rot Damaged Surface Percentage Using Hybrid Linear Discriminant Analysis and

Decision Tree." In *2021 International Conference on Intelligent Technologies (CONIT)*, pp. 1-6. IEEE, 2021.

[35] Alajas, Oliver John, Ronnie Concepcion, Elmer Dadios, Edwin Sybingco, Christan Hail Mendigoria, and Heinrick Aquino. "Prediction of Grape Leaf Black Rot Damaged Surface Percentage Using Hybrid Linear Discriminant Analysis and Decision Tree." In *2021 International Conference on Intelligent Technologies (CONIT)*, pp. 1-6. IEEE, 2021.

[36] Gupta, Bhumika, Aditya Rawat, Akshay Jain, Arpit Arora, and Naresh Dhami. "Analysis of various decision tree algorithms for classification in data mining." *International Journal of Computer Applications* 163, no. 8 (2017): 15-19.

[37] Kherif, Ferath, and AdeliyaLatypova. "Principal component analysis." In *Machine Learning*, pp. 209-225. Academic Press, 2020.

[38] Ghosh, Joyoshree, and Shaon Bhatta Shuvo. "Improving classification model's performance using linear discriminant analysis on linear data." In *2019 10th International Conference on Computing, Communication and Networking Technologies (ICCCNT)*, pp. 1-5. IEEE, 2019.

[39] Djarum, Danny Hartanto, Zainal Ahmad, and Jie Zhang. "River Water Quality Prediction in Malaysia Based on Extra Tree Regression Model Coupled with Linear Discriminant Analysis (LDA)." In *Computer Aided Chemical Engineering*, vol. 50, pp. 1491-1496. Elsevier, 2021.

[40] Hou, Yun (2018), "KEEL dataset repository," *Mendeley Data*, V1, doi: 10.17632/py4hhv3rb8.1.

Chapter 6

Image Steganography Using Deep Neural Networks

Reddy Madhavi K.[1,*], **PhD**
K. Pranitha[2], **M. Tech**
Nagendar Yamsani[3], **M. Tech**
Mohmad Ahmed Ali[4], **M. Tech**
K. Srujan Raju[5], **PhD**
and Balijapalli Prathyusha[6], **B. Tech**

[1]School of Computing, Mohan Babu University, Tirupati, India
[2]B.V. Raju Institute of Technology, Narsapur, Medak, Telangana, India
[3]Assistant Professor, School of Computer Science and Artificial Intelligence,
SR University, Warangal, India
[4]Associate Professor, Department of CSE, CMR Institute of Technology, Hyderabad, Telangana, India
[5]Professor, Department of CSE, CMR Technical Campus, Hyderabad, Telangana, India
[6]UG Scholar, CSE, Sree Vidyanikethan Engineering College, Tirupati, A.P., India

Abstract

Steganography involves the use of hiding a secret or unknown message in a regular message. Steganography is commonly used in such a way that smaller messages are difficult to detect within a larger image's noisy areas. In this chapter, we try to fit a color image in another image which is of the same size. Deep Neural Networks (DNN) are trained to simultaneously produce the concealing and disclosing activities in a pair-wise fashion. The system is tested on real-world photos from a range of

---

[*] Corresponding Author's Emai: kreddymadhavi@gmail.com.

In: Information and Knowledge Systems
Editors: Manaswini Pradhan and Satchidananda Dehurl
ISBN: 979-8-89113-303-7
© 2024 Nova Science Publishers, Inc.

sources and was trained on images chosen at random from the ImageNet collection. Beyond illustrating how deep learning may be used to successfully hide images, we closely study the process and consider extensions. Many methods such as Least Significant Bit (LSB), Highly Undetectable steGO (HUGO), Wavelet Obtained Weights (WOW) are effective for image steganography but they encrypt the secret message in the carrier image's Least Significant Bits, in contrast to the Deep Neural Network method, which compacts and spreads the representation of the secret image throughout all of the available bits. Without being expressly instructed to do so, the deep neural network algorithm examines the data for features that correlate and combine them to support learning in a faster way. This is the most advanced technique which is used for the image steganography.

Keywords: steganography, LSB, HUGO, WOW, deep neural networks

Introduction

The growth of network security and multimedia has made people's daily lives and jobs much more convenient, but it has also revealed an increasing number of security flaws. For example, in the case of trade secrets, personal privacy, and even military defense security, the repercussions of a leak of classified information are immense. Information steganography has attracted an increasing amount of interest and research in recent years as a means of addressing the issues in the realm of data protection. Image Steganography (Chandan et al., 2020) is the method of hiding the unknown image within the host image by using a few aspects of the host image. The detector detects no abnormalities while the host image is being sent. Finally, the receiver can receive the hidden image in a secure manner from the sender. The traditional methods used for the image steganography (Sunitha et al., 2021) is "Least Significant Bit" and "Highly Undetectable steGo", though these methods work faster and easy to implement, but they are insecure and can easily cause suspicion.

In this research, the Deep Neural Networks are used for image steganography. Process of image stegnography is shown in Figure 1. A image whose resolution is lower is encoded into a image which has higher resolution using the "LSB" method. Deep neural networks, on the other hand, are used for the encoding and decoding of several hidden images inside a single cover image of the same resolution. In contrast to simple feed-forward, fully connected networks in image steganography, DNNs are able to tackle much more complex issues and are very safe. Two network modules - the "Hiding Network" and "Extraction Network" are a part of this deep neural network paradigm. The convolution operation used by the "Hiding Network" to blend the enciphered image into the host image and send the hidden result to the receiver is then used by the "Extraction Network" to derive the encrypted image. It is capable of finally learning from its own errors. It can check the veracity of its findings or results, and make any necessary revisions.

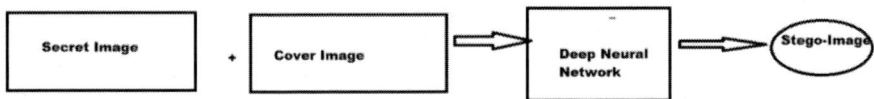

Figure 1. Process of Image Steganography.

Relevant Review

The "Elliptic Curve- El Gamal (EC-El Gamal) Cryptography" and "Chaotic Theory" are the foundations of an (Luo et al., 2019) unique asymmetric picture encryption technique that is developed. Performance comparisons and experimental analysis show that the suggested method has significant ability to withstand a chosen-plaintext attack, high security, and good efficiency, making it have potential approaches for image dependable communications. Lu, Wei et al., 2019, put out a half-tone picture steganographic system that intends to produce stego images with excellent Steganography scheme can accomplish high statistical anti-steganalysis security with superior visuals without lowering embedding capacity. The global fusion module (GFM) incorporated the multi-scale features (Jiang et al., 2020) from various HDB's for a worldwide fusion and representation. The fusion maps are then realigned and sub-pixel up-sampled to produce the final profile-enriched residual map. Comprehensive experimental findings on based on standard datasets and seriously reduced images demonstrate that their model beats advanced approaches with regard to objective measurements and plausible visual effects, and also benefits from a quick and accurate reconstruction. A novel U-Net-based image steganography system was presented by (Duan et al., 2019). The experimental findings demonstrated that the suggested technique spreads and compresses the information of the hidden image which is embedded across all the bits in cover image, which improves embedding capacity and addresses the issue of obvious visual cues. a method for concealing secret messages was developed that maps various steganographic techniques to complicated texture objects. Firstly, complex texture regions are chosen using an Object Detection Algorithm. Second, three various steganographic techniques were employed to conceal the secret message within the chosen block region. The results of the experiments showed that the approach improves safety and toughness. Two upgraded RDH methods based on dual imaging are proposed: Reversible pixel pair LSB matching based on dual stego images and modified LSB matching based (Sahu et al., 2019) on dual stego images. Both the proposed methods have demonstrated that both RS and PDH attacks are resistant to anti-steganalytic abilities. Hiding of images within images (Baluja et al., 2019) and to protect highly secured (Rasras et al., 2019) images.

Proposed Method

Steganography is especially intriguing for applications where encryption cannot be used to safeguard the transfer of sensitive information. In order to overcome the existing drawbacks due to LSB and HUGO, the deep neural network is proposed, the model is trained and tested against a dataset. It gave good accuracy by correctly making outputs/predictions. The design of Deep Neural Network is represented in Figure 2. The basic design of a DNN is made up of an input layer, one or more hidden layers, and the result layer. Each layer is made up of neurons, which are processing units that perform a specific computation on their input.

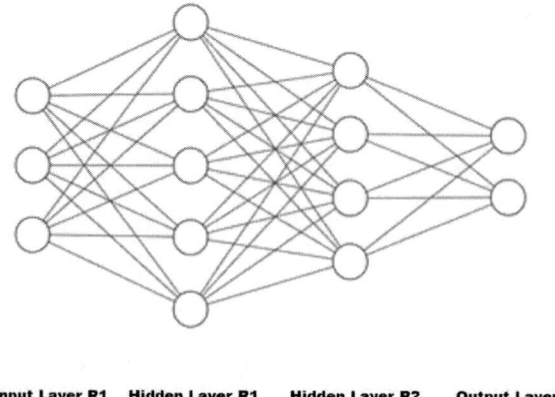

Figure 2. Architecture of DNN.

The spatial space processes change the cover image's pixel bit values to place the restricted data. The mystery bits are simply assembled in the pixel bytes of cover image. The goal is to pictorially conceal the entire NxN pixel from the hidden image in another cover image with as little distortion as possible. The input data is a cover image which is given to the DNN (Kreuk et al., 2019) model, each neuron in the input layer could represent a pixel value. The hidden layers are responsible for transforming the input data into a representation that is more useful for the result/output layer. The data of the cover image from the input layer is taken into a "byte array". Bitstream of the original image file is recovered into other "byte array" using this "byte array". The original image is created once aforementioned "byte array" is written into decoded file. The output layer is responsible for producing stego image for the input given. The figure 3 shows the model for image steganography using deep neural networks. It consists encoder and decoder networks.

Encoder network: It consists of a prep network, which corresponds to input for a unknown image. The cover image is produced by the prep network, then supplied into the hiding network.

Decoder Network: The decoder network is made up of reveal networks that have been trained to decode the associated message.

Prep Network: The Prep Network consists of a combination of two layers. Each layer is composed of three distinct Conv2D layers. This trio of Conv2D layers has size of the kernel as of 3, 4, and 5 for each layer. The length of the stride was measured along the both axes which consistently stays at 1. Each Conv2D layer receives the proper amount of padding in order to maintain the final image's dimensions.

Hiding Network: The hidden network is composed of five layers, every layer of these is composed of the three different "Conv2D Layers". The Conv2D levels in the prep network and the "Conv2D Layers" in the hidden network have a basic structure that is similar.

Reveal Network: With 5 layers of identically shaped Conv2D layers, every one of this network has a similar to the hidden network's underlying structure.

The outcomes of hiding a secret image over a single cover image are shown in Figure 3. The outputs of the encoder network are shown on the left, the input image is displayed in the left corner. The secret photos are not revealed by the encoded cover image, which is quite the original cover's style. The encoded cover image which looks similar to the cover image is transmitted through a decoder network. Cover and secret images showin in Figure 4 and deep stegnography process in Figure 5. The secret message is decoded by the decoder network. The secret image is retrieved successfully.

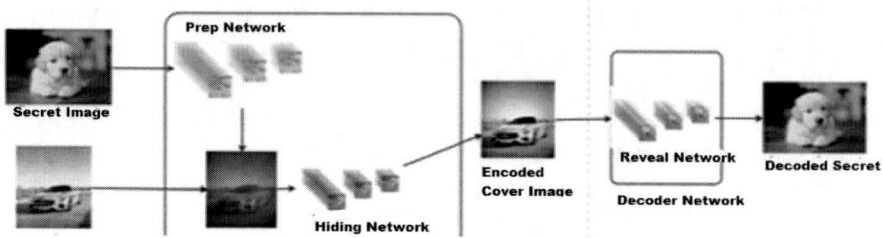

Figure 3. Model for Image Steganography using DNN.

Results and Discussion

The experimentation is done in a stepwise manner:

- Step 1: The ImageNet dataset containing of cover images and their corresponding stego-images
- are loaded.
- Step 2: Preprocess of the images in the dataset are done, which may include normalization and resizing. Preprocessing the dataset is a crucial step as it may contain missing data, outliers and the data need to be cleaned concerning to improve the quality of the model.
- Step 3: The architecture of the deep neural network is defined, which typically consists of convolutional layers and fully- connected layers. The main challenges and dataset will determine the number of layers and the size of each layer.
- Step 4: The weights and biases of the Deep Neural Network are randomly initialized.
- Step 5: The following steps for each training example are repeated:
    a. Initially, the cover image and corresponding stego image are loaded.
    b. Forwardly propagated the cover image through the network, using the current weights and biases.
    c. The error between the predicted output and the stego image is calculated.

d. Backpropagated the error through the network, updating the weights and biases using gradient descent.
- Step 6: The steps from 1 to 5 are repeated for a specified number of epochs, or until the network reaches a desired level of accuracy.
- Step 7: The performance of the network is evaluated on a separate validation set.
- If the performance is not satisfactory, adjust the hyperparameters of the network and repeat from step 4.

Additionally, various regularization techniques such as "Ridge Regression (L2 Norm)", "Lasso (L1 Norm) Dropout" are used to prevent overfitting of the network to the training data. Finally, the proposed model gave an accuracy of 98% and it is significant to evaluate the execution of the network on a different test set to guarantee that it can accurately detect steganography in unseen images.

Figure 4. Cover Image & Secret Image.

Figure 5. Deep Steganography Process.

The DNN model for Image Steganography is evaluated against ImageNet Dataset and it gave a good accuracy. In Figure 6, it is shown that DNN performed well on the ImageNet Dataset compared to CNN model. Accuracy of the Deep Neural Network algorithm used for Image Steganography is 97 percent, it is accurate than Convolutional Neural Network Model. It is able to embed secret information within an image without affecting its visual quality as shown in Figure5, the accuracy, precision, recall and F1-score of CNN Model and DNN can be found in Table 1.

Table 1. Results of CNN and DNN models

Model	Accuracy	Precision	Recall	F1-Score
CNN	0.959	0.964	0.980	0.972
DNN	0.98	0.987	0.995	0.989

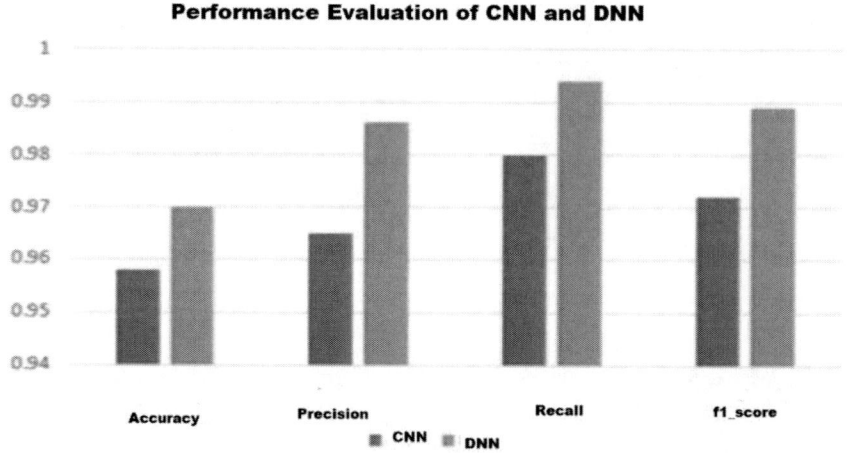

Figure 6. Graph showing the performances of CNN and DNN.

Accuracy Score is calculated by Number of Correct Predictions / Total Prediction Number.

The robustness of the DNN model is high compared to Convolutional Neural Networks model that is the DNN model can withstand various attacks, such as image manipulation or compression, and still be able to extract the hidden information correctly. The DNN model learns end-to-end, meaning that the entire steganography process can be learned in a single step. This makes the process more efficient and less prone to errors. The DNN-based steganography algorithm is able to measure the quantity of unknown data that can be inserted into a image without affecting its visual quality.

Extensions of the work

We plan to further extend the project with more secret images. To recover the encoded image with the least amount of loss, we intend to modify the model. We plan to expand the field of image steganography by using GANs or even deeper neural networks.

Conclusion

We have understood Steganography in the image domain. With the aid of a deep neural network algorithm, we have proposed the steganography technique in the current work. When compared to current methods, the suggested framework yields outcomes that are much better. Steg-Expose is a tool that can determine whether anything has been hidden in a photograph. If the image is edited and covered up using current techniques, it is actually quite straightforward to tell. Python has been used to implement the suggested task, which even demonstrates very little code execution time. This suggests that the treatment is highly effective and quick. We looked at a brand-new approach to enhance the best possible outcomes of steganography. This opens up a tremendous variety of extra opportunities. It should be feasible to achieve the equivalent for many media, such as audio and video. Moreover, using smaller privileged insights on larger covers will help the prep + conceal net provide far better results.

Disclaimer

None

References

Baluja, Shumeet. "Hiding images within images." *IEEE transactions on pattern analysis and machine intelligence* 42, no. 7 (2019): 1685-1697.

Chandhan, Madhavarapu, K. Reddy Madhavi, U. Ganesh Naidu, and Padmavathi Kora. "A NOVEL GEOTAGGING METHOD USING IMAGE STEGANOGRAPHY AND GPS." *Turkish Journal of Physiotherapy and Rehabilitation* (2020) 32: 3.

Duan, Xintao, Kai Jia, Baoxia Li, Daidou Guo, En Zhang, and Chuan Qin. "Reversible image steganography scheme based on a U-Net structure." *IEEE Access* 7 (2019): 9314-9323.

Jiang, Kui, Zhongyuan Wang, Peng Yi, and Junjun Jiang. "Hierarchical dense recursive network for image super-resolution." *Pattern Recognition* 107 (2020): 107475.

Kreuk, Felix, Yossi Adi, Bhiksha Raj, Rita Singh, and Joseph Keshet. *"Hide and speak: Towards deep neural networks for speech steganography."* arXiv preprint arXiv:1902.03083 (2019).

Luo, Yuling, Xue Ouyang, Junxiu Liu, and Lvchen Cao. "An image encryption method based on elliptic curve elgamal encryption and chaotic systems." *IEEE Access* 7 (2019): 38507-38522.

Lu, Wei, Yingjie Xue, Yuileong Yeung, Hongmei Liu, Jiwu Huang, and Yun-Qing Shi. "Secure halftone image steganography based on pixel density transition." *IEEE Transactions on Dependable and Secure Computing* 18, no. 3 (2019): 1137-1149.

Rasras, Rashad J., Ziad A. AlQadi, and Mutaz Rasmi Abu Sara. "A methodology based on steganography and cryptography to protect highly secure messages." *Engineering, Technology & Applied Science Research* 9, no. 1 (2019): 3681-3684.

Sahu, Aditya Kumar, and Gandharba Swain. "Dual stego-imaging based reversible data hiding using improved LSB matching." *International Journal of Intelligent Engineering and Systems* 12, no. 5 (2019): 63-73.

Sunitha, Gurram. "Intelligent System to Find the Health Care Centers for Senior Citizens Based on Disease and Nearest Locations using GPS." *Turkish Journal of Computer and Mathematics Education (TURCOMAT)* 12, no. 2 (2021): 2140-2150.

Xiao, Yi, Xinqing Wang, Peng Zhang, Fanjie Meng, and Faming Shao. "Object detection based on faster R-CNN algorithm with skip pooling and fusion of contextual information." *Sensors* 20, no. 19 (2020): 5490.

Chapter 7

Machine Learning on the Farm Animal Health Care System: A Review

**Goddeti Mallikarjun[1]
and V. A. Narayana[2,*], PhD**

[1]Department of CSE, JNTUH, Kukatpally,Research Centre,
CMR College of Engineering and Technology, Hyderabad, Telangana, India
[2]Department of CSE, CMR College of Engineering and Technology,
Hyderabad, Telangana, India

Abstract

Improving farm animal production is becoming increasingly important in addressing food insecurity in the modern world, as the global population grows and also profit can be made by raising farm animals. Improving farm animal health may boost productivity and profit. This review looks at the application of machine learning technology in farm animals' health monitoring systems. Different chemicals have been used in live stock's food to improve muscle and milk production, hence latest technology is required for livestock welfare. Machine learning is an essential study subject because it discovers patterns in massive amounts of data. The latest technologies, like machine learning, will help the farmer diagnose the farm animal's disease with reasonable accuracy. Animals are easily affected by diseases due to different factors, such as environmental conditions. Machine learning algorithms are mainly classified into two types: unsupervised and supervised. Unsupervised algorithms work with labeled data and unlabeled data, Unsupervised algorithms are used to group (clustering) the input into a big data set. In contrast, supervised algorithms use labeled data to train algorithms,

---

*Corresponding Author's Email:g.mallikarjun@cmrcet.ac.in.

In: Information and Knowledge Systems
Editors: Manaswini Pradhan and Satchidananda Dehurl
ISBN: 979-8-89113-303-7
© 2024 Nova Science Publishers, Inc.

categorize data, and forecast output. Machine learning algorithms/technologies are already being used in many human health care industries to predict diseases such as heart disease; thus, considering these assists in increasing livestock production (e.g.: milk and meat) and generating profit.

Keywords: livestock, farm animals, machine learning, unsupervised, supervised, dataset

Introduction

Adequate proteins are needed for human metabolism. Animal-derived protein often has a superior quality for humans due to its amino acid composition and easy digestion (Ibrahim Elmadfaand Alexa L, 2017). The world population is growing at a rapid speed. As per www.worldometers.info, the world population is 8,000,000,000+ (November, 2022), and India's population is 1,412,683,683+ (November, 2022) with the world population's food insufficiency also increasing rapidly. People are unable to obtain enough protein-rich food due to the population's rapid development.

Since there is still the same amount of area available for raising animals, population growth outpaces productivity. Utilizing the most recent technologies in animal husbandry is essential to reducing the global food crisis, particularly in countries like India. In a few years, India will surpass China as the most populous nation, but technology usage is not increasing at the same rate. Livestock husbandry is important to India's rural economy and has an impact on both the domestic and global economies. Livestock farming makes a major contribution to the socio-economic system; approximately 62% of farmers are associated with livestock farming (Arghyadeep Das1, 2020).

The world is in stimulating times where machine learning has an intense influence on comprehensive applications, especially in the healthcare sector. Machine learning uses big data technologies and high-performance computing to create new opportunities to understand the data-intensive process (Konstantinos G. Liakos, 2018). Welfare assessment is pivotal in animal farming; behavior is a crucial indicator in animal welfare assessment. With the help of machine learning technology, farmers can detect their behavior continuously and automatically. Monitoring the behavior of animals will help predict diseases. Hence, farmers can take action to improve animal welfare (N. Lia, Z. Ren†, 2019). In a country like India, which is the top milk producer in the world, the use of the latest technology in livestock production is mandatory. This review paper analyzes the latest machine learning technologies to help in animal farming by improving health and productivity.

Overview of Machine Learning

One of the major trending branches in artificial intelligence is machine learning, which is used in a wide variety of applications; This problem-solving ratio has increased. Especially in the health sector, the use of machine learning is increasing progressively, and ML helps to improve disease prediction and progression. For example, many machine-learning applications have been used in cardiology to improve workflow and overcome the limitations of traditional methods (Tim Smole, 2021). If you observe the types of algorithms in machine learning, there are four types.

1) Supervised.
2) Unsupervised.
3) Semi-supervised.
4) Reinforcement.

Supervised: Supervised algorithms learn from the labeled data to predict the outcome; The name itself says under supervision, meaning it works under the supervision and needs to train the machine before applying this algorithm. It deals with labeled data. It is divided into two categories.

i) Regression
ii) classification

Unsupervised: No supervision is required here; it works on unlabeled data and finds hidden patterns and insights in the given data. It learns from past experiences, like humans. It is categorized into two types.

i) Clustering
ii) Association

Semi-supervised: To overcome the disadvantages of the unsupervised algorithm, this algorithm is introduced. Here the data is a combination of labeled and unlabeled, but part of the labeled data is small.

Reinforcement: It is a feedback-based learning technique in which these agents learn the behavior from the action and based on the results. The agents learn automatically based on feedback from their actions, and here there is no concept of labeled data (Ayon Dey, 2016).

Farm Animal Growth Ratein India

It is important to note that increasing the number of animals in a confined area may not be a sustainable solution, as it could lead to overcrowding and poor animal welfare, as well as an increased risk of disease spread. Furthermore, clearing more land for farming animals can have negative environmental impacts such as deforestation and loss of biodiversity. The census shows the growth rate of livestock in India depicted in table 1.

Using technology to identify animal infections at an early stage is a promising solution that can benefit both animal welfare and food security. By detecting and treating diseases early, farmers can prevent the spread of disease and avoid the economic losses associated with sick animals. Additionally, early detection of diseases can help ensure the safety of the food supply and prevent the spread of zoonotic diseases that can affect human health.

Advances in technologies such as artificial intelligence, machine learning, and genomic sequencing have made it possible to develop new tools for disease detection and management in livestock. These technologies can be used to monitor animal health, identify potential disease outbreaks, and track the spread of disease within a herd or population.

Table 1. The growth rate of livestock in India

Category	Population (In millions) 2012	Population (In millions) 2019	% growth
Cattle	190.90	192.49	0.83
Buffalo	108.70	109.85	1.06
Sheep	65.07	74.26	14.13
Goat	135.17	148.88	10.14
Donkey	0.32	0.12	-61.23
Camel	0.40	0.25	-37.05

Technology in the Farm Animal Health Care System

Remote monitoring: Remote monitoring systems collect data on animal behavior, health, and performance using sensors and other equipment. This information may be wirelessly communicated to a central database, where it can be examined and deployed to identify possible health issues before they become serious.

Precision livestock farming: Precision livestock farming collects data on individual animals' behavior, health, and performance using a variety of sensors, cameras, and other equipment. This data is then examined using artificial intelligence (AI) and machine learning (ML) algorithms to detect possible health problems before they become serious. This technology also aids in the optimization of feed, water, and other resources in order to increase animal welfare and production.

Robotics: Robots are employed for a variety of duties in livestock health care, ranging from feeding and watering animals to cleaning stalls and cages. These robots are outfitted with sensors and cameras to monitor the health and behavior of the animals, and the data is utilized to make choices about feeding and watering regimens.

Use of Machine Learning in the Farm Animal Healthcare System

Disease detection: Machine learning algorithms may be trained to recognize patterns in animal behavior, such as changes in feeding or drinking habits or aberrant movements that may suggest the development of sickness. This can assist farmers in detecting infections early and taking the necessary actions to prevent their spread.

Environmental monitoring: Machine learning may be used to monitor environmental elements like temperature, humidity, and air quality, which can have an impact on cattle health and welfare. Machine learning algorithms can notify farmers of possible concerns, such as changes in temperature or humidity levels.

Feed optimization: Data on animal feed intake and growth rates may be analyzed using machine learning, allowing farmers to optimize feed formulas and decrease waste. This can increase animal health while also saving producers money.

Predictive Modeling: Machine learning may be used to create prediction models that assist farmers in anticipating disease outbreaks and taking preventive measures. A model might be developed, for example, to forecast the possibility of an epidemic of a certain illness based on characteristics such as weather patterns and animal behavior.

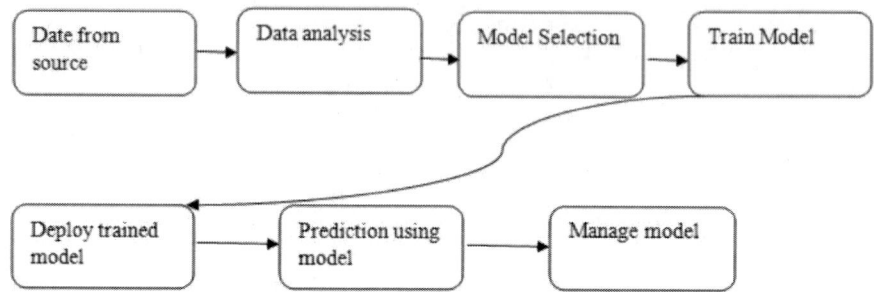

Figure1. Sample workflow of a machine learning model.

The basic machine learning workflow is illustrated in Figure 1. To address any problem using machine learning, the first step is to gather raw data from the source, then evaluate the data based on the requirements, and then train the model. The following phase in the workflow is to deploy the model, which has already been trained, and then forecast using the model. The final step is managing the machine learning model.

Literature Review

Animal Health Diagnosis Using Machine Learning

(K.L. Reagan et al., 2019), applied machine learning algorithms in the diagnosis of hypoadrenocorticism in dogs, ML tools are more powerful in the diagnosis of the condition. Here, the use of the boosted tree ML algorithm produced better accuracy than other tools; machine learning algorithms need to be applied to a wide array of patients.

Interoperable Data in Animal Farming

(Christiane Bahlo etal., 2019) made use of rich data that would assist farmers in improving farming, and farmers prefer model outputs, such as recommendations, over data. As a result, decision-making and output forecasting tools should be provided. A good set of queryable geoinformation has the capacity to develop better livestock models. There is a need for machine learning algorithms to filter the predictive functionality.

Animal Digestion System Using a Machine Learning Model

(QiangFuaet et al., 2020) used the Tradition model, which requires assumptions and is a parametric model. A machine learning model does not require any assumptions, it is a non-parametric model. The advantage of this model is that it's suitable for complex systems. Artificial intelligence and machine learning need to be applied more in the dairy industry.

Use of Machine Learning in Classification

(Rodrigo Garcia etal., 2020) determined that utilizing machine learning techniques to improve categorization in cattle husbandry is necessary, Ensemble learning, which has previously shown success in other contexts, may be used to combine numerous models to accomplish this improvement. This challenge can be thought of as "semi-supervised" or "meta-learning."

Analyzing Animal Movement and Behavior Using Machine Learning

(Eloise S. Fogarty etal., 2020) applied a few machine-learning technologies to analyze animal behavior. There is no protocol to analyze the data accurately, especially in animal behavior classification. Accuracy varies depending on the selection of the machine learning algorithm. Future research needs to consider active epochs and the use of best behavior detection technology.

Table 2 is a comparison of machine learning techniques that are already being applied to analyze the food and behavior of animals. Here are some machine learning technologies compared with limited data sets.

A supervised algorithm such as Support Vector Machine will regulate a hyperplane that leverages the border of the two datasets to construct an orator sovereign cross justification framework, and the trials that sit on the boundary are referred to as support vectors (Narayana V.A., 2018). Machine Learning Supervised algorithms are used in data classification and image classification. Using such algorithms as SVM and convolutional neural networks (CNN) in image classification will boost accuracy while decreasing computation time (Suresh Merugu, 2021). And the Nave Bayes (NB) algorithm is good at text-based categorization. Using NB methods provides good accuracy of up to 98% when compared to other machine learning algorithms (Merugu S, 2019).

Table 2. Comparisons of the latest ML techniques used to analyze the behavior and grazing of animals

Reference	ML technique used	Dataset	Accuracy
Eloise S. Fogartya(2020)	SVM	prediction of grazing, lying, standing andwalking(30z epoch)	75.6%
F.A.P. Alvarenga(2020)	decision-tree algorithm	Behavior (sheep)	96.6%
Duy Ngoc Do(2022)	Random Forest	Aleutian disease	96.2%
SafitFirmansyah(2020)	Naïve Bayes Algorithm and Genetic Algorithm	Diagnose Cattle Disease	95%

Proposed Methodology

Sensor data may be used to enhance preventative healthcare, environmental monitoring, feed optimization, and predictive modeling using machine learning.

Temperature, humidity, air quality, feed intake, water consumption, and animal movement are just a few of the elements that sensors may assess. Machine learning algorithms can then analyze the data to identify patterns and correlations that humans may not see. These algorithms may be trained to spot patterns that suggest possible health issues, such as changes in feed intake or movement patterns that may indicate an illness's beginning.

The proposed methodology will take the input data from the sensors and cameras, and raw data collected from animal farms will be sent to clustering. Clustering will be performed by an unsupervised algorithm, it is a process of dividing the data into groups. A cluster of data will be sent for classification, which will be performed by the supervised algorithm. It is the process of understanding and recognizing data and also performs the grouping of data effectively, as shown in Figure 2. Clustering the data before classification will help to perform the classification effectively, and it will help to increase the accuracy in predicting the disease of animals, preventative healthcare. The output may be a warning to the farmer that a certain animal is showing indications of sickness, along with treatment or isolation advice.

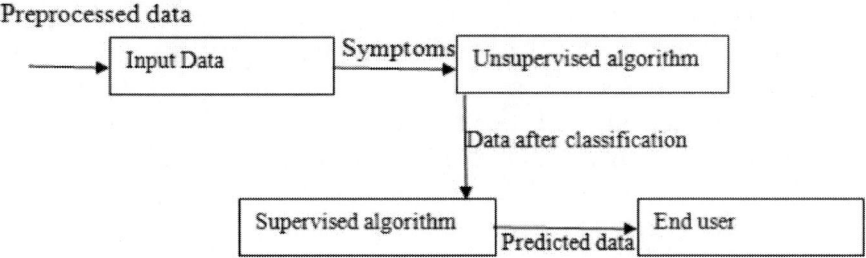

Figure 2. Methodologyto Predict Animal Diseases.

Future Work

The use of machine learning or new technologies in diagnosis farm animal disease is in its infant stage. The employment of technology in agriculture and livestock farms is particularly inadequate in India. This work has already covered a few algorithms that are already employed in livestock farming in limited settings to diagnose animal behavior, but those tests have not been satisfactory. The objective is to create or implement an appropriate ML system to forecast animal illness with high accuracy, taking into account meteorological conditions. One of the main challenges is collecting and managing large amounts of data on animal health, environmental conditions, and other relevant factors. This data can be collected through a variety of methods, including sensor networks, remote sensing, and manual observations, but it requires careful management and analysis to extract useful insights.

Another challenge is developing and testing accurate machine learning algorithms that can effectively diagnosis animal disease outcomes based on this data. This requires a deep understanding of both the biology of the animals and the statistical methods used in machine learning.

Conclusion

Emerging technologies help fuel farming. In a real-life situation like COVID-19(corona) pandemic farmers were restricted from visiting farms, and livestock farming, where 24/7 monitoring is required. With the help of technology, farmers can easily get out of these scenarios. The adoption of new technologies like ML will provide insights into farm animals' consumption, production, and activity. Modern technologies like ML will start playing an emphatic role in livestock farming. Predicting livestock illness allows farmers to farm more animals in the same area, increasing the utilization of the area and productivity. As a result, using livestock technology to mitigate food shortages will be critical. Predicting farm animal illnesses will assist farmers in increasing production and revenues. While there are still some unanswered problems and restrictions, discovering the power of contemporary animal farming technology is requisite.

References

Arghyadeep Das1, Raju, R. and NeelaMadhavPatnaik, Present Scenario and Role of LivestockSector in Rural Economy of India: A Review. 2020., *International Journal of LivestockResearch,* 10.5455/ijlr.20200701051344.

Ayon Dey,Machine Learning Algorithms: A Review,2016.*(IJCSIT) International Journal of Computer Science and Information Technologies,* Vol. 7 (3), 2016, 1174-1179.

Christiane Bahloa, Peter Dahlhausa, Helen Thompsona, Mark Trotter, *The role of interoperable data standards in precisionlivestockfarming in extensive livestocksystems: A review*,2019.

Duy Ngoc Do, Guoyu Hu, PouryaDavoudi, AlimohammadShirzadifar, GhaderManafiazarand Younes Miar, *Applying Machine Learning Algorithms for the Classification of MinkInfectedwithAleutianDiseaseUsingDifferent Data Sources*,2022.https://doi.org/10.3390/ani12182386.

Eloise S. Fogartya, David L. Swaina, Greg M. Croninb, Luis E. Moraesc, Mark Trottera *Behaviour classification of extensivelygrazedsheepusing machine learning*,2020. https://doi.org/10.1016/j.compag.2019.105175.

Alvarenga F.A.P., I. Borges, V.H. Oddy, R.C. Dobosb, *Discrimination of biting and chewingbehaviour in sheepusing a tri-axialAccelerometer*,2020.https://doi.org/10.1016/j.compag.2019.105051.

Ibrahim Elmadfaand Alexa L. Meyer, *Animal Proteins as Important Contributors to a Healthy Human Diet*. 2017. doi: 10.1146/annurev-animal-022516-022943.

Reagan K.L., B.A. Reagan, C. Gilor, Machine learningalgorithm as a diagnostic tool.forhypoadrenocorticism in dogs,2019. https://doi.org/10.1016/j.domaniend.2019.106396.

Konstantinos G. Liakos, Patrizia Busato, DimitriosMoshou, Simon Pearson and DionysisBochtis, Machine Learning in Agriculture: A Review, 2018.*Sensors*2018, 18, 2674;10.3390/s18082674.

Merugu S., Reddy M.C.S., Goyal E., Piplani L. (2019), Text Message Classification UsingSupervised Machine Learning Algorithms. In:Kumar A., Mozar S. (eds) *ICCCE 2018*.https://doi.org/10.1007/978-981-13-0212-1_15.

Narayana, V.A., Chamakura, A., Gandi, R., "Deceptive call recognition in a network using machine learning,"*Acta Technica CSAV* (CeskoslovenskAkademieVed), 2018, Vol. 63-Issue 6, PP-909-914.

Lia N., Z. Ren†, D. Li and L. ZengReview:Automated techniques for monitoring the behaviour and welfare of broilers and layinghens: towards the goal of precisionlivestockfarming,2019. doi:10.1017/S1751731119002155.

QiangFua, WeizhengShena, XiaoliWeia, YonggenZhangc, HangshuXinc, ZhongbinSua, Chunjiang Zhao, *Prediction of the dietenergy digestion using kernel extremelearningmachine: A case studywith Holstein dry cows*, 2020.https://doi.org/10.1016/j.compag.2020.105231.

Rodrigo García, Jose Aguilar, Mauricio Toro, Angel Pinto, Paul Rodríguez,*A systematicliteraturereview on the use of machine learning in precisionlivestockfarming*,2020. https://doi.org/10.1016/j.compag.2020.105826.

SafitFirmansyah, EndangSugiharti, RizaArifudin, *Optimization of Naïve Bayes Method usingGeneticAlgorithm to Diagnose CattleDisease*,2020.

Suresh Merugu, AnujTiwari&Surendra Kumar Sharma, (2021), Spatial–Spectral Image Classification with Edge Preserving Method, *Journal of the Indian Society of RemoteSensing*ISSN 0255-660X *J.Indian Soc.Remote Sens*.https://doi.org/10.1007/s12524-020-01265-7.

Tim Smole, Bojan Zunkoviˇc, MatejPiˇculin, EnjaKokalj, Marko Robnik-ˇSikonja, MatjaˇzKukar, Dimitrios I. Fotiadis, Vasileios C. Pezoulas, Nikolaos S. Tachos, Fausto Barlocco, Francesco Mazzarotto, DejanaPopoviˊc, Lars Maier, Lazar Velicki, Guy A. MacGowan, IacopoOlivotto, NenadFilipoviˊc, Djordje G. Jakovljeviˊc, Zoran Bosniˊc, A machine learning-basedrisk stratification model for ventriculartachycardia and heartfailure in hypertrophiccardiomyopathy,2021. https://doi.org/10.1016/j.compbiomed.2021.104648.

Chapter 8

Social Media Behavior Prediction Using Sentiment Analysis

Kurakula Arun Kumar[1,*]
Sanjana Maankar[2,†]
K. Sai Sahithi[2,‡]
P. Tharun Sai Reddy[2,#]
and K. Srujan Raju[3,§]

[1]School of Computing, Mohan Babu University, Tirupati, Andhra Pradesh, India
[2]Department of CSE(AI), Sree Vidyanikethan Engineering College, A.P., India
[3]Department of CSE, CMR Technical Campus, Hyderabad, India

Abstract

Social media platforms provide valuable data that can be used to anticipate customer behavior. By analyzing post, comment, likes, and offers, it is possible to gain insights into their interests and motivations. For instance, if a customer sends a friend request to another user, the receiver can be prompted to indicate whether they accept the request or not based on the requester'sblocked status and the reason for the block. Before accepting a friend request, it is possible to analyze the requester goals by examining their postings and comments. By leveraging trade mark research data, it is feasible to predict the direction of customer behavior before they initiate a friend request. Additionally, it is possible

---

[*] Corresponding Author's Email: k.arunjoy@gmail.com.
[†] Corresponding Author's Email: sanjanamaaankar17@gmail.com.
[‡] Corresponding Author's Email: ksaisahithi20@gmail.com.
[#] Corresponding Author's Email: tarun33.reddy@gmail.com.
[§] Corresponding Author's Email: ksrujanraju@gmail.com.

In: Information and Knowledge Systems
Editors: Manaswini Pradhan and Satchidananda Dehurl
ISBN: 979-8-89113-303-7
© 2024 Nova Science Publishers, Inc.

to monitor customer posts and comments and analyze them in detail to gain deeper insights into their behavior.

Keywords: social media, customer behavior, natural language processing, machine learning, trademark research data

Introduction

People use Facebook to express their opinions on various topics. Given the enormous amount of data generated by posts and comments, it is expected that Facebook can effectively analyze this data. The aim is to develop a system that can classify each post based on its sentiment, including emotions such as anger, shock, joy, fear, annoyance, and sentimentality. Facebook login page is shown in Figure 1. This research investigates the use of feature-based approaches and bag-of-words techniques to represent words, enabling the categorization of social media posts based on their sentiment.

Information Collection: Rather than having exact queries generate our results, our data is an impressionistic representation of enthusiastic remarks. This type of data handling with hand- stamped analysis allows us to cross-check, detect differences, and assess classifiers. Natural Language Processing takes on the challenge of distinguishing emotions with various levels of detail. The initial step is to classify files by level. They recommend combining verbal elements like the shout stamp, affiliation, supplement, and shout tags with verbal features like a retweet, hashtags, earlier explicit purpose of words, and POS of words. Our successes rely on previous decisions made; analyzing feelings is seen as a tactic.

Evaluation procedure: This assignment features a two-cover layout with two categories of slant farthest points: positive and negative. The word appears frequently in both favorable and negative comments, according to a preliminary analysis. Depending on the uncontrolled context in which they appear, words can have varying levels of centrality. This method also searches the content for any diagrams that might contain information useful in understanding collections. The compiled guidelines for jokes in the context of the length data cannot be compared to another dataset, like Facebook. The paper's remaining fragments are dealt with as follows.

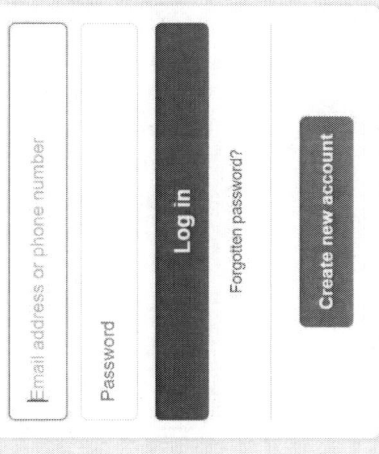

Figure 1. Facebook login page.

Approaches for Sentiment Classification

Supervised Learning   Unsupervised Learning

1. Decision tree Classifiers
2. Linear classifiers
   a. support vector machine
   b. neural networks
3. Rule-base classifiers
4. Probabilistic classifiers
   a. Navie Bayes
   b. Bayesian network
   c. Maximun entropy

1. Clustering
2. Association
3. Anomaly Detection
4. Dimensionality Reduction
5. Autoencoders
6. Generative Models

Literature Review

(Kadambari et al., 2015) explores how Twitter can be used for trend analysis and data mining. With the increasing popularity of multimedia and mobile devices, people are more connected than ever and are sharing their opinions on public forums, blogs, and social networking sites. Twitter has become a major platform for users to share their thoughts and ideas, with millions of tweets being generated every second, providing a constant stream of real-time data. (Agarwal et al., 2011) conducted a study on the use of sentiment analysis techniques for Twitter data, and their findings demonstrated that tweets can be accurately classified as positive, negative, or neutral. The study also looked into the use of features such as emoticons and hashtags for sentiment analysis. Sentiment analysis, also known as opinion mining, is a field that involves identifying and extracting subjective information from textual data.

(Rashkin et al., 2017) proposed a multilingual approach to sentiment analysis that centered on connotation frames in social media data. The authors developed a dataset of pre-defined connotation frames, which are sets of words that represent different sentiments, and employed it to train a model for targeted sentiment analysis. The use of connotation frames enhanced the accuracy of sentiment analysis, particularly in multilingual settings. The authors demonstrated the potential of their approach for forecasting shifts in public sentiment over time. The applications of sentiment analysis in social media are numerous and include understanding public opinion, predicting trends, and developing effective marketing strategies. (Rangkuti et al., 2018) investigated sentiment analysis of movie reviews by using ensemble features and feature selection methods based on Pearson correlation. The authors experimented with several features including bag-of-words, part-of-speech tags, and sentiment lexicons to classify reviews into positive, negative, or neutral categories.

(Zhao et al., 2018) applied deep convolutional neural networks (CNN) for sentiment analysis on Twitter data. The authors proposed a deep CNN model that leverages the spatial structure of text data, including word embeddings and character embeddings, to classify tweets as positive, negative, or neutral. The model achieved high accuracy in sentiment analysis tasks, outperforming traditional machine learning algorithms and other deep learning models. Rai and Gupta (2013) investigated the potential of social media networks for the rural population of India. The authors argued that rural India has remained largely untouched by the benefits of social media, and that social media networks have the potential to empower rural communities and connect them to the larger world. The authors discussed the challenges of adopting social media in rural areas, including limited access to technology and low literacy rates.

(Miller et al., 1999) emphasizes the importance of understanding user behavior when designing interactive systems. They argue that designers should consider users' cognitive and emotional states, expectations, and goals. The article reviews the literature on behavioral issues in the use of interactive systems and discusses how factors such as task complexity, interface design, and user experience can affect user behavior. The authors stress the need for user testing and evaluation to identify potential usability issues and ensure the system meets user needs. They provide examples of evaluation methods and discuss the importance of a user-centered approach to design to create effective and efficient interactive systems that meet users' needs and goals. (Thong et al., 2002) article aims to explore the factors that affect user acceptance of digital libraries, emphasizing the importance of understanding these factors for designing effective digital libraries that meet users' needs and increase adoption. Through a comprehensive literature review, the authors identify three key factors that affect user acceptance: interface characteristics, organizational context, and individual differences. They examine how ease of use and usefulness of the interface, level of support and resources provided by the organization, and individual characteristics such as computer self-efficacy and perceived enjoyment can shape users' perceptions and attitudes towards digital libraries.

Methodology

The Natural Language Processing project has looked into the evaluation of sentiment on multiple levels. Generally, categorization tasks are seen as binary issues, with the option of ither positive or negative. However, this project has gone further and also considered three-way classifications, such as positive versus negative versus neutral, and positive versus negative. A feature analysis that identifies the most fundamental features Basic aspects to take into account is the quantity of positive qualifiers and negative verbs. The combination of tree bits with senti-features has a slight edge over unigrams with senti-incorporates, while all other features are insignificant. The most often used classifiers, such as SVM and Navie Bayes. Facebook posts that include uproar, for instance, include prolonged words, pronouns that can't be detected, sentences that are broken apart, and words that are organized. Hashtags are one special feature that is detected and handled appropriately. Process of web application is shown in Figure 2. Words can convey similar or opposite meanings. Word polarities are identified. Both uninspiring and motivational demeanors can be distinguished based on the extreme.

Algorithm

Given a set of data points D, and a point P to classify, the algorithm for naive Bayes is as follows:

1. For each feature F in P, calculate the probability $P(F|C)$, where C is the class of the data point. This is the probability that the feature would be observed, given the class.
2. Once all probabilities have been calculated, multiply them together to get $P(P|C)$, the probability of observing the point P, given the class C.
3. Repeat the above steps for each class, to get $P(P|C1)$, $P(P|C2)$, etc.
4. Finally, calculate $P(C|P)$, the probability of the point P belonging to the class C, using the formula

$P(C|P) = P(P|C) * P(C) / P(P)$, where $P(C)$ is the prior probability of the class.

Examining User Postings and Comments

Considering an interpersonal structure, we focus on the simplest scenario with two choices (A and B) based on a snippet of data. For example, the data could be a comment in a comment box, with A as reposting and B as not. We can predict which clients will be affected by the data at a given time by analyzing the diffusion rate. Accept that the customer in this enterprise kept a close eye on every neighbor's behavior to gather all the information. Prior to service, information about the clients is recorded. Natural handling calculation is used to predict the clients' mental state.

This formula generates summaries of key points in content/docs, arranges content in predetermined classes and style sheets builds the page with an app page, login page, and friend req. acknowledgment page. When a customer logs in with a mail ID, all is recorded on-site page.

Analysis of Sample Data

Barbosa & Feng (2010) created a model using extreme expectations from 3 sites as loud markers, & 1000 physically tagged tweets for tweaking & testing. They don't say how they compiled the data. It is suggested to use features such as the extremity of words and POS (parts of speech) of words in combination with features like tweets, hashtags, links, punctuation, and emotion stamps. Our research results demonstrate that combining the extremity of words with their respective parts of speech produces the best results in terms of classifier performance. The tweet's structure emphasizes assistance, but only marginally. We present highlights that outperform unigram models & look into an alternative method of information portrayal, with physically verified data free from bias. Unlike precise questions, we have gushing tweets & cross-approval trials to check classifier exec. over folds. Tree part presentation performs optimally & consistently across models, without precise highlight planning.

Figure 2. Block Diagram

Vital Role of Sentiment Analysis

Emotional analysis is critical to learn customers' likes/dislikes & commitments. Gathering & understanding their feelings is essential. Platforms like Twitter/Facebook provide data & hyperlinks related to certain topics. Gaining knowledge on web hosting user actions such as clicking and posting URLs offers insight into digital communication, consumer profiling and more. Prior to our approach, much link-sharing data was inaccessible due to its exclusive and confidential characteristics. We will explain our approach and present two perspectives in the following sections. Weanalyzed multiple variables (freq., spread, layout) of posting-based views to understand user behavior. System activity was limited (e.g., Facebook), and it was tough to evaluate user link usage with system access (e.g., Twitter). Our dataset had URLs from one/multiple accounts, some sporadic, others recurrent. We identified characteristics to distinguish user posting styles.

Posting User Network

We are curious about the total number of posts on Facebook during our inquiry, which may indicate the connection objective and the sharer's goal. We analyze user behavior to examine if malicious URLs can be detected in online social networks and if posting or snap-based techniques are effective. These indicators are thought to be harder to manipulate than post content or a website's main page, offering more reliable long-term detection.

Barriers in Virtual Communities and Structure of Social Media

At present, the prevalence of online platforms such as Facebook, Twitter, Google+, LinkedIn, and Foursquare has become widespread and they have become an integral part of many people's daily routines. People use traditional computers and mobile devices to access OSNs, with over one billion users worldwide. In this review, we analyze the questions related to customer leads in OSNs from multiple angles, beginning with client cooperation and social networks. We also study movement action from a systems perspective. Additionally, as cell phones become commodities, we concentrate on the characteristics of social practices in a variety of contexts. Each node in a family tree represents a service recipient, and edges indicate connections between them. Wilson et al., analyze data scraped from Facebook to determine if social ties can be used as customer collaboration evidence. Results show users often interact with a small group regularly and have no communication with up to half of their friends, showing OSNS ties cannot compare to real-world family. Connection graphs, better than family trees, are used for anti-spam and Sybil protection, and Renren data (42m users, 1.66b conns) supports weak connections leading to strong collaboration. Three conclusions: passive interaction is more successful than active engagement; natural relationships are not consistent; level of fame unrelated to posting frequency or close friends, even for highly popular.

Connecting Multiple Users

Research with limited capacity poses a challenge of quickly increasing social diagram size with customer number. To represent such charts, diagram testing techniques are used. Despite being widely employed as a part of social chart investigation, it has been found that the effects of Breadth-First Search (BFS) and Random Walk (RW) are biased to higher-degree vertices. MHRW & RWRW perform reliably on Facebook [6], & exam process uses online joining diagnostics to assess test quality. FS w/multidimensional RW reduces estimation errors vs RW, esp. for disconnected or loosely connected diagrams. Types of client activities can't be represented in a chart; admins can screen data & interpret OSN use. Examining a static dataset to assess an OSN presents difficulties. Dynamic data collection & analysis of info, commonality & spatial dependence helps. Facebook uses server farms for global supportNon-U.S. users experience slower response times; the Internet has unnecessary activity; long-distance travel is affected by interpersonal organizations, while short-distance travel is composed of both stable short-term growth and transient fluctuating growth; irregular direct contact reveals 50-70% of growth, while social relations only 10-30%; a model of human adaptability considering transient growth is presented.

Widely Used Networks

Smart devices create PSNs w/ adaptability. Effective guiding practices are essential to manage, taking into account comments, and inquiry words. User social structure, and collaboration affect guiding norms. Air pocket Rap transmits PSN data via social media using two metrics, pinpointing audience & dispersing messages to influential nodes. Analysis shows BUBBLE Rap has similar conveyance to other strategies, using fewer assets. A framework produces similarity rating by detecting common features & actions of two people's profiles, informing them someone nearby could be interested. Context is taken into account; the next event can be forecasted. Social structure & communication of users of intelligent devices influences way regulations are implemented.

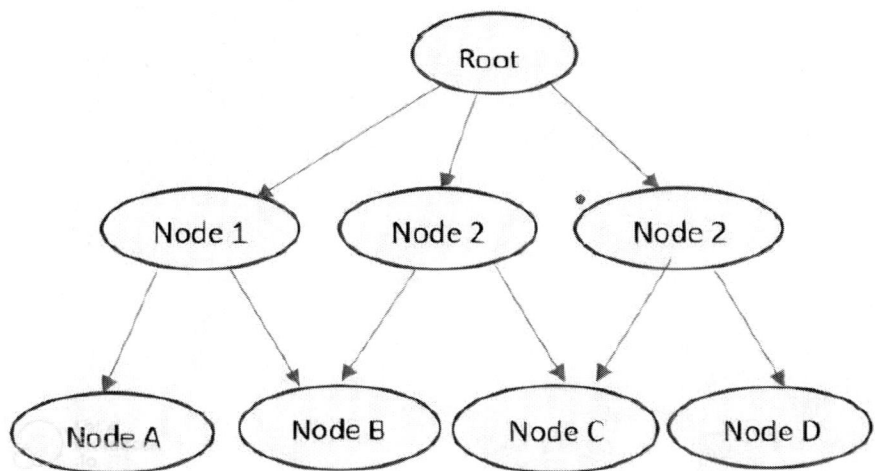

Figure 3. Network Design.

Major OSN plats have mobile apps; we research MSN client practices. Data limits click-stream info and idle clients' behaviour; info from certain ISPs recorded. Social charts show user interaction, but limited data may not show all activities. Admin can screen data based on user OSN use. Design of Network is shown in Figure 3. We investigate OSN client behavior in this region; swift info collection, chart analysis and dynamic info objects challenge data storage and increase pressure, requiring trustworthy role models for cooperation.

Result Analysis

Sentiment score with respect to the frequency are shown in Figure 4 and sentiment analysis of facebookposts are shown in Figure 5.

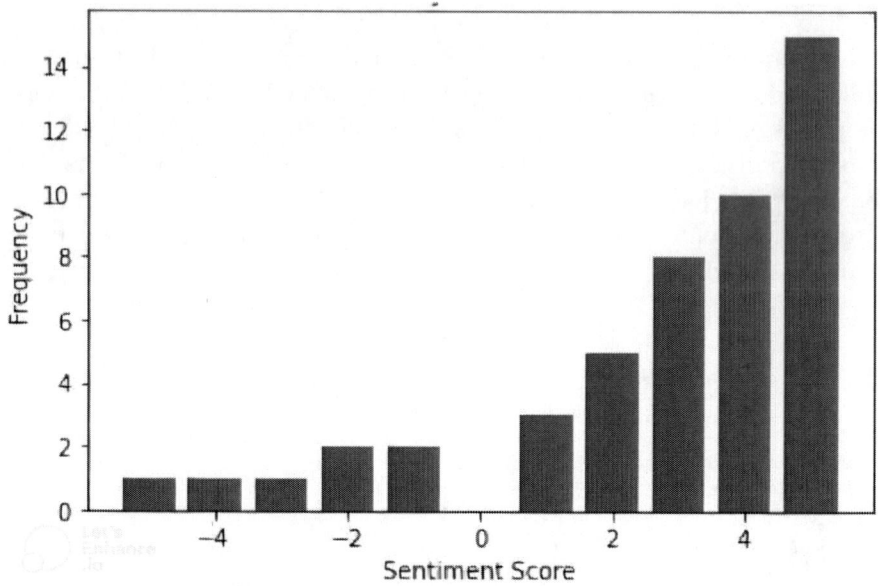

Figure 4. Sentimental Analysis of tweets on twitter.

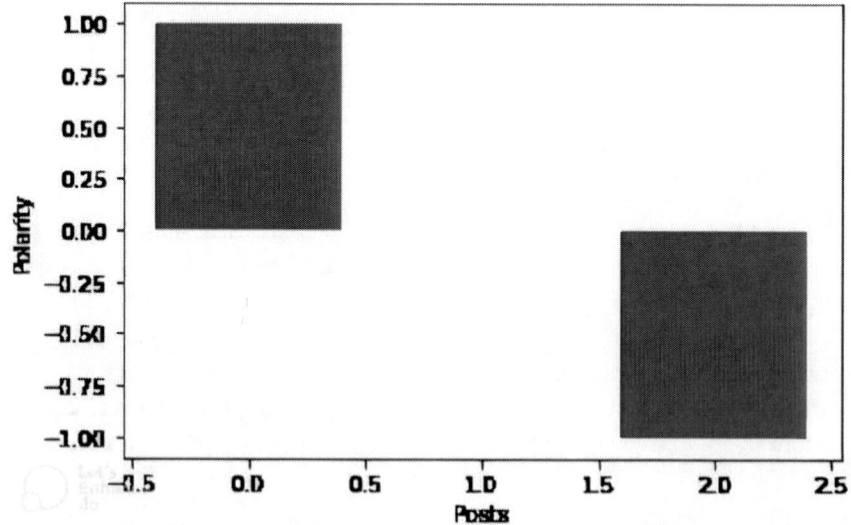

Figure 5. Sentimental Analysis of Facebook posts and comments.

Conclusion

Analyse the existing admin structure and suggest potential directions for the future. To meet the needs of system providers, master communities, and end users, we anticipate this review will enhance the customer experience from different perspectives. Taking the context and customer perspectives into account in various applications is critical. Further research on context-based SA is therefore required. TL techniques provide a way to apply related knowledge to the environment. Scientists are now utilizing NLP tools to optimize SA, though there is still room for improvement.

References

Agarwal, Apoorv, Boyi Xie, Ilia Vovsha, Owen Rambow, and Rebecca J. Passonneau. "Sentiment analysis of twitter data." In *Proceedings of the workshop on language in social media (LSM 2011)*, pp. 30-38. 2011.

Jianqiang, Zhao, Gui Xiaolin, and Zhang Xuejun. "Deep convolution neural networks for twitter sentiment analysis." *IEEE access* 6 (2018): 23253-23260.

Kadambari, Sanchita, Kalpana Jaswal, Praveen Kumar, and Seema Rawat. "Using twitter for tapping public minds, predict trends and generate value." In 2015 Fifth International Conference on Advanced Computing & Communication Technologies, pp. 586-589. *IEEE*, 2015.

Miller, Lance A., and John C. Thomas Jr. "Behavioral issues in the use of interactive systems." *International journal of human-computer studies* 51, no. 2 (1999): 169-196.

Rai, Gupta Anmol, and Zafar Shahila. "Rural India: the next frontier for social media networks." *International Journal of Engineering Research & Technology* 2, no. 1 (2013): 1-6.

Rakheja, Shivani, Neelam Saxena, and Seema Rawat. "Evolution and Upliftment of Rural India Using Social Media." In 2018 International Conference on Computational Techniques, Electronics and Mechanical Systems (CTEMS), pp. 533-538. *IEEE*, 2018.

Rangkuti, Fachrul Rozy Saputra, M. Ali Fauzi, Yuita Arum Sari, and Eka Dewi Lukmana Sari. "Sentiment analysis on movie reviews using ensemble features and pearson correlation based feature selection." In 2018 International Conference on Sustainable Information Engineering and Technology (SIET), pp. 88-91. *IEEE*, 2018.

Rashkin, Hannah, Eric Bell, Yejin Choi, and Svitlana Volkova. "Multilingual connotation frames: a case study on social media for targeted sentiment analysis and forecast." In *Proceedings of the 55th Annual Meeting of the Association for Computational Linguistics* (Volume 2: Short Papers), pp. 459-464. 2017.

Thong, James Y. L., Weiyin Hong, and Kar-Yan Tam. "Understanding user acceptance of digital libraries: what are the roles of interface characteristics, organizational context, and individual differences?." *International journal of human-computer studies* 57, no. 3 (2002): 215-242.

Biographical Sketches

K. Arun Kumar
Affiliation: Mohan Babu University
Education: PhD
Business address: AsssistantProfessor, School of Computing, Mohan Babu University, Tirupati, Andhra Pradesh, India. Pincode- 517102
Research and Professional experience: 15 years
Professional Appointments: Life Member of IEI

Sanjana Maankar
Affiliation: SVEC
Education: B.Tech
Business address: Sree VidaynikethanEngineeering College, Tirupati, Andhra Pradesh, India. Pincode- 517102

K. Sai Sahithi
Affiliation: SVEC
Education: B.Tech
Business address: Sree VidaynikethanEngineeering College, Tirupati, Andhra Pradesh, India. Pincode- 517102

Tharun Sai Reddy
Affiliation: SVEC
Education: B.Tech
Business address: Sree VidaynikethanEngineeering College, Tirupati, Andhra Pradesh, India. Pincode- 517102

K. Srujan Raju
Affiliation: JNTUH
Education: Ph.D

Business address: CMR Technical Campus, Kandlakoya Village, Medchal, 501401

Research and Professional experience: Research experience is: 10+ years, Professional experience is: 20+ years

Professional Appointments: CSI, International Association of Engineers

Honors: Jyesta Acharya Award, Sarvotham Acharya Puraskar, Best faculty of the year, CSI Excellent contribution award

Publication from Last 3 years: 27

Chapter 9

Ultra-Wide Band Electromagnetic Band Gap (EBG) Antenna with WIMAX, WLAN and Satellite Downlink Communication Band Notching

Pakala Raveendra Babu[1,*] and Rama Krishna Dasari[2]

[1]Research Scholar, ECE, University College of Engineering,
Osmania University, Hyderabad & Associate Professor,
ECE, CMR College of Engineering & Technology, Hyderabad, India
[2]Professor of ECE, University College of Engineering,
Osmania University, Hyderabad, India

Abstract

A monopole UWB antenna with three bands notching that can be turned off WiMAX operates between 3.3 and 4.0 GHz, whereas WLAN operates between 5.1 and 5.8 GHz and satellite downlink communication operates between 7.2 and 7.8 GHz. Tapered transitions are utilised to match the impedance between 2.7 and 13.4 GHz between rectangular patches and feed lines. Electromagnetic Band Gaps (EBGs) structures with fractal and two via edge-located (TVEL) characteristics were created by etching an open loop slot into the radiating patch, which was then connected to a faulty microstrip structure (DMS) frequency bands now come in three levels. The proposed antenna is made out of RT/duroid 5880 and is 32360.8 mm^3 in size. VSWR is 2 offers impedance bandwidth from 2.9 to 11.2 GHz, with the exception of the notched bands. The antenna was designed to provide almost Omni-directional

---

[*] Corresponding Author's Email: praveendrababu@cmrcet.ac.in.

In: Information and Knowledge Systems
Editors: Manaswini Pradhan and Satchidananda Dehurl
ISBN: 979-8-89113-303-7
© 2024 Nova Science Publishers, Inc.

emission patterns and a consistent gain over the whole UWB frequency range that was requested. To investigate the impedance and radiation properties of the UWB antenna, it was developed, modelled, constructed and tested between the simulated and measured data; there is a high level of agreement. According to the findings, the proposed UWB applications may benefit from this antenna.

Keywords: UWB Monopole Antenna, Electromagnetic Band Gaps (EBGs) structures, two via edge-located (TVEL) Triple band notched Defected microstrip structure, open loop slot & omni-directional

Introduction

Ultra-wideband systems are of particular interest to researchers because to the many advantages associated with their utilisation (Singh, A. P., R. Khanna, and H. Singh, 2017). These advantages include High capacity, low power, low cost, and interference-free deployment. The UWB works at frequencies ranging from 3.1 GHz to 10.6 GHz. IEEE 802.a WLAN operates between 5.15 and 5.35 GHz and between 5.7825 and 5.725 GHz, as well as sending messages back to the satellite (7.25–7.75 GHz) are all compatible with UWB technology, which operates at a frequency of 3.3–3.6 GH (Yadav, A., M. D. Sharma, and R. P. Yadav, 2019). Band-stop filters increase system size and cost, but it may be possible to lower these frequencies by using such filters (Rehman, S. U. and M. A. S. Alkanhal, 2017). Researchers want a small UWB antenna with notch properties for more than one band.

UWB antennas with band-notching capabilities are made in several ways. Radiating patch and ground plane have U-shaped, U-shaped with parasitic strips, C-shaped, and inverted U-shaped slots. Various types of resonating slots have an effective length of around half a wavelength (Shaik, L. A., C. Saha, J. Y. Siddiqui, and Y. M. M. Antar, 2016). The use of a slot to generate band-notch features is a useful strategy. Multiple slots may be used to provide multi-band notch features, however they have an influence on the antenna's gain, efficiency, and radiation pattern (Jaglan, N., S. D. Gupta, B. K. Kanaujia, and S. Srivastava, 2018). To generate band-notch characteristics, Resonator structures are also feasible (Like an electric ring resonator or a split ring resonator). It's hard to come up with these plans. EBGs are now in more buildings EBG structures have been used to lessen the impact of surface waves and other undesired reactions, hence improving the performance of antennas (Vendik, I. B., A. Rusakov, K. Kanjanasit, J. Hong, and D. Filonov, 2017). A "notch" in the band was created in a UWB antenna by using EBG structures in its construction. On a substrate measuring 38 by 40 millimetres single CLV-EBG and ELV-EBG construction makes a band-notch UWB antenna. UWB antennas employ CLV-EBG and ELV-EBG components, even though the substrate is bigger (B Premalatha, PR Babu, G Srikanth, 2021, Raveendrababu, 2022 & 2023 Yazdi, M. and N. Komjani, 2011). A 42.50 mm² circular UWB antenna has two notches made by four CLV EBG structures. In this study, two EBG designs are used to make a small UWB antenna with a notch for three bands like WiMAX and X band notches use a structure called TVEL-EBG WLAN, on the other hand, uses a structure called fractal EBG (Yazdi, M. and N. Komjani, 2011, B Premalatha, G Srikanth, PR Babu, MV Sonth, 2020). The antenna was planned, modelled and built. Using electromagnetic full-wave simulations, it was shown that the antenna worked well. Wave simulations were done with HFSS (Premalatha, B., Prasad, M. V. S., Murthy, M. B. R., 2018, Yang, F. and Y. Rahmat-Samii, 2003).

Antenna Design and Geometry

UWB Antenna

Figure 1 depicts the designed and simulated EBG antenna. The RT/duroid 5880 substrate, which is 0.8 mm thickness is used in the antenna's construction4. The Figure 2 represents the proposed antenna geometry with dimensions as mentioned in Table 1.

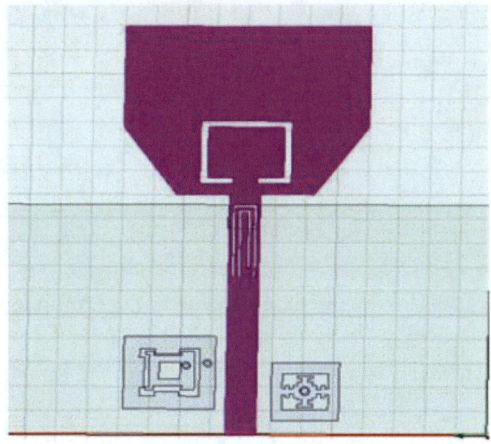

Figure 1. Simulated Antenna with EBG.

Table 1. Dimensions of proposed antenna

Parameter	L_1	L_2	L_3	L_4	L_5	L_6	L_7
Value(mm)	5.6	5.2	14	20	4.8	5.6	6
Parameter	L_8	L_9	W_1	W_2	W_3	W_4	W_5
Value(mm)	2	19	16	6	5	3.5	1.6
Parameter	W_6	W_7	W_8	W	L	d	
Value(mm)	12	2	2	32	36	0.2	

The following elements make up the UWB antenna layout: a standard patch antenna with Figure 3 shows a part of the ground plane, is constructed to display UWB behaviour between 3.1 and 10.6 GHz (case I) (a). Figure 4 depicts the VSWR of this antenna, which indicates that it works between 3.5 and 6.5 GHz with a VSWR less than 2. As shown in Figure 1, a radiator with a tapered transition (case II) may improve UWB antenna matching (b). The suggested antenna's VSWR demonstrates that it can operate between 3.1 and 11 GHz (UWB applications). Because of this, the ground plane has been given the addition of a basic rectangular hole (case III).

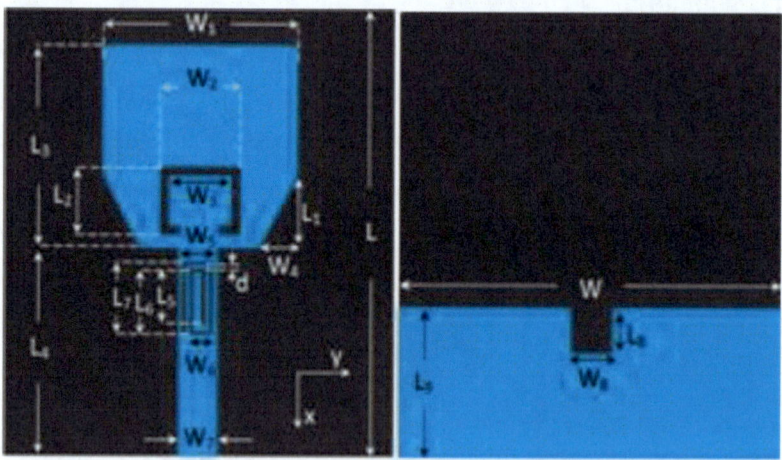

Figure 2. The suggested UWB antenna's geometry (a) Front view (b) back view.

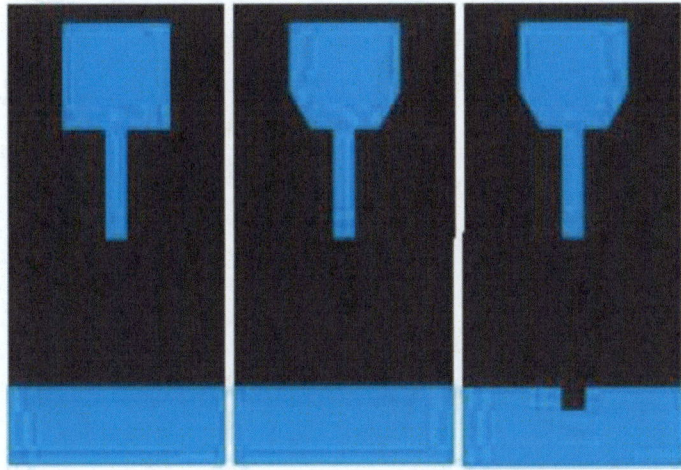

Figure 3. Top and bottom UWB antenna configurations (a) Case I (b) Case II (c) Case III.

Filter size and complexity are reduced thanks to DMS. Boosting stopband attenuation, it minimises radiation loss (Premalatha, B., Prasad, M. V. S., Murthy, M. B. R., 2018). A two-dimensional DMS filter is seen in Figure 4. Incorporate microstrip lines. This slot alters the capacitance and inductance of the microstrip line, causing band-stopping. To attain the right resonance frequency, the DMS filter was resized. The Figure 5 shows the Return loss, S11 of proposed antenna without EBG and S11< -10 dB between 3.1 GHz to 10.6 GHz, it indicates the antenna operating in UWB band range.

Figure 4. The layout of DMS band stop filter.

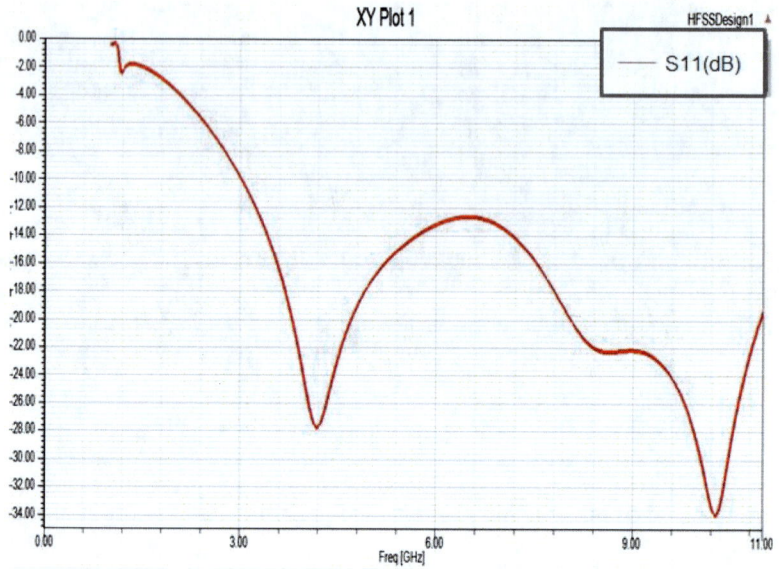

Figure 5. S Parameters of UWB antenna without EBG structures.

EBG Structures

EBG structures produce a thin, periodic pattern of tiny metal patches over dielectric surfaces to block particular frequency bands of electromagnetic radiation. Two EBG structures are employed in this work. The first is the TVEL (Two Via Edge Located) EBG structure, while the second is the Fractal EBG structure (Premalatha, B., Prasad, M. V. S., Murthy, M. B. R, 2018).

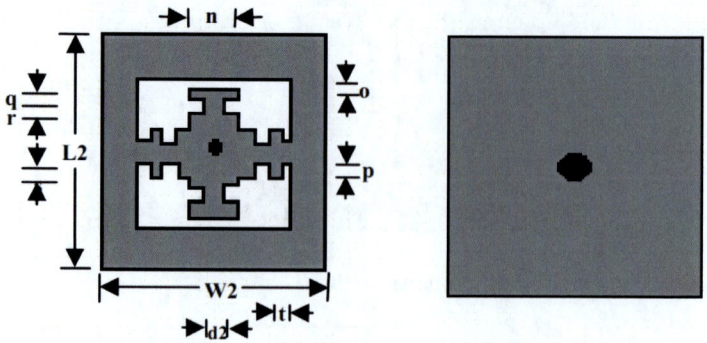

Figure 6. (a) Fractal EBG (b) Conventional Mushroom EBG.

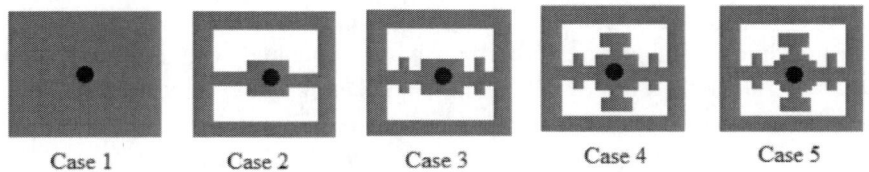

Figure 7. Fractal EBG structure evolution.

Fractal EBG Evolution

A typical square EBG that looks like a mushroom is 0.10 inches by 0.10 inches, where 0 is the centre band notch frequency free space wavelength. 4.4 mm-4.8 mm fractal EBGs should be smaller than conventional EBGs. Figure 6 shows the fractal EBG unit element and the traditional mushroom-type EBG with the same dimensions. WLAN frequency ranges 5.6 to 6.2 GHz are rejected by the classic EBG structure, but the fractal EBG rejects 5.15-5.8 GHz WLAN frequencies. Regular EBG is 11% larger than fractal EBG. In addition, its wideband notch properties are better than those of standard EBG.

Its W2 is 4.44 mm, the length of the L2 is 4.8 mm, the n is 0.25 mm, the O is 0.02 mm, the P is 0.25 mm, the Q is 0.03 mm, the R is 0.25 mm, the s is 0.25 mm, the t is 0.25 mm, and the D2 is 0.94 millimetres. The fractal EBG evolution is shown in Figure 7. Fractal EBG increases surface current density and inductance decreasing metal surface area (Jaglan, N., B. K. Kanaujia, S. D. Gupta, and S. Srivastava, 2017). The impedance of the fractal EBG is considerably greater. Fractal EBGs create capacitance as a result of the space between the strips of metal. Because capacitive impact is stronger than inductive effect, fractal EBG's impedance is higher (B Premalatha, G. Srikanth, P. R. Babu, M. V. Sonth, 2020).

Two Via Edge Located (TVEL) EBG Evolution

Figure 8 illustrates the proposed TVEL EBG as well as the conventional TVEL EBG. Two EBGs have a unit element size of 6.6 mm2. TVEL EBG rejects the proposed antenna's Frequencies in the WiMAX band (3.4-4.4 GHz) and the X band (7.2- 7.7) GHz spectrum. C and L are increased to make a compact EBG. Figure 8 shows the TVEL EBG's progression. To enhance the surface area of a metal while minimising inductance, metallic strips are used.

As the space between slots decreases, capacitance increases. Both the outer and inter-metallic rings contribute to the frequency of the notch in the lower band (B. Premalatha, P. R. Babu, G. Srikanth, 2021). When the number of slots gets closer together, the capacitance goes up, but the inductance goes down. The fundamental frequency of the notch in the lower band drops. The frequency of the notch is determined by the inner metallic ring, because the inner ring's slot dimensions are set, capacitance remains constant, but inductance drops. Hence, the upper band notch's centre frequency increases (Yang, F. and Y. Rahmat-Samii, 2003). The step by step process of TVEL EBG evolution is shown in Figure 9. As a result, the bottom and upper band notches may be altered by modifying the construction of TVEL EBG. W1 = 6 mm, L1 = 6 mm, a = 1 mm, b = 1.6 mm, c = 1.3 mm, e = 3.2 mm, f = 3.9 mm, g = 0.88 mm, h = 1.84 mm, I = 0.55 mm, j = 2.5 mm, k = 3.9 mm, m = 1.38 mm, l = 0.324 mm, d = 7.88 mm.

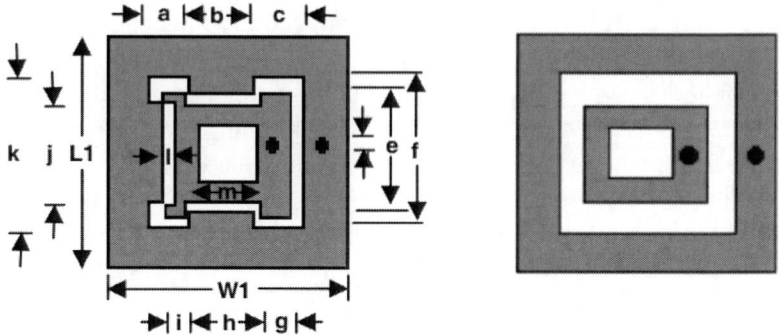

Figure 8. Geometries of EBG (a) Proposed TVEL EBG (b) Conventional TVEL EBG.

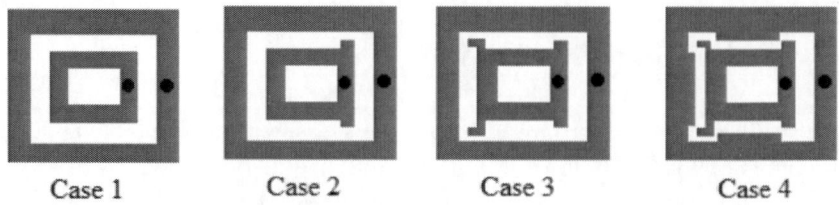

Figure 9. Evolution of TVEL EBG structures suggested.

Effect of Position of EBG Structures

In EBG structures, the feed line is capacitive connected to the structure. When the feed line connects to the EBG structures at the centre band notch frequency, the antenna stops responding. The capacitive coupling decreases as the distance between the EBG structure grows, and the middle band's centre band notch frequency increases owing feed line and fractal EBG capacitance reduction. Increasing The farther away the feed line is from the fractal EBG, the worse the band notch characteristics and the lower the maximum VSWR, as shown in Figure 10.

The lower band notch is unaffected by changes in the feed line-to-TVEL EBG distance. Capacitance, on the other hand, rises in proportion to the increase in distance. Reduced inductance may be achieved by reducing the surface current on the metallic strip that surrounds the core.

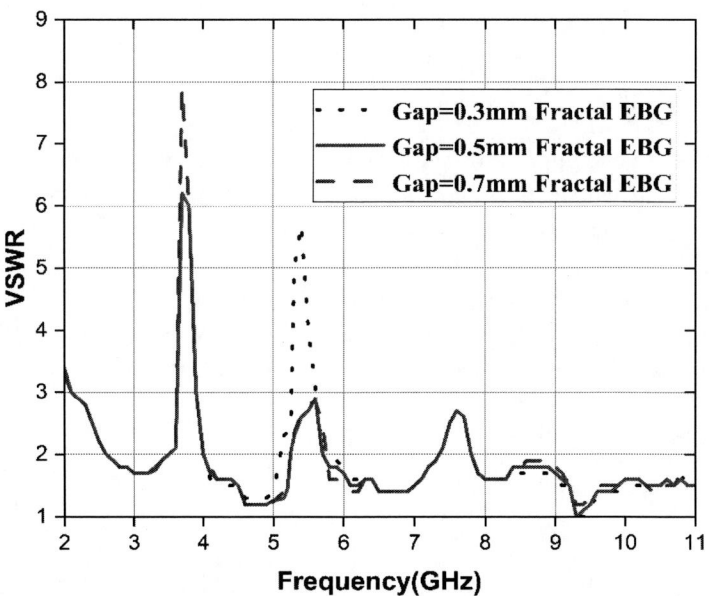

Figure 10. VSWR of gap between fed line and Fractal EBG.

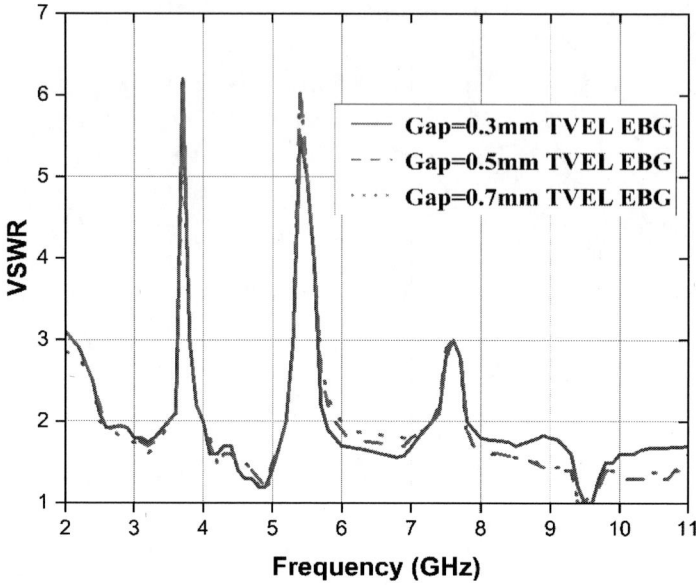

Figure 11. VSWR of gap between fed line and TVEL EBG.

As the gap gets bigger, the centre frequency of the notch in the lower band goes up. As the gap gets bigger, surface current and inductance go down. Figure 11 shows that the upper band notch frequency increases with feed line and TVEL EBG distance. Due to EBG buildings' closeness to feed lines, they may be used to give the necessary band notches in different UWB antennas. Figure 12 demonstrates that simulation in eigen-mode solution confirms the bandgap properties of the EBG cell.

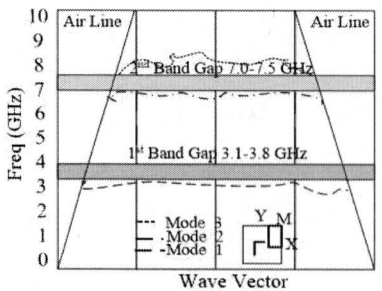 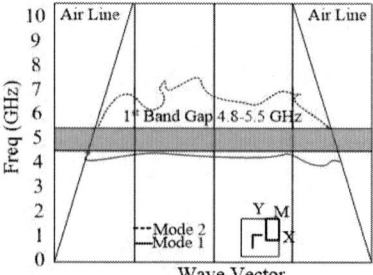

Figure 12. Dispersion diagram for (a)TVEL EBG (b)Fractal EBG.

Figure 13. Photographs of fabricated antenna (a) Top view (b) bottom view.

Physical Antenna

The simulated antenna has been fabricated with the substrate of RT/duroid 5880 as shown in Figure 13 and the Antenna parameters like Return loss & Group delay of the antenna was measured, the measured results was compared with simulated antenna.

Results and Discussion

The proposed RT/duroid 5880 substrate EBG antenna with triple band notches at 3.65 GHz (3.3–4.0 GHz), 5.45 GHz (5.1–5.8 GHz) and 7.5 GHz (7.2–7.4 GHz) respectively has designed using HFSS tool. The measured and simulated results are consistent. The surface current distribution is shown in Figure 14 for three distinct centre notched frequencies: 3.65 GHz, 5.45 GHz, and 7.5 GHz. The band notch is indicated by At 3.65 GHz, 5.45 GHz and 7.5 GHz. In the TVEL-EBG structure, there is a lot of surface current and at 5.45 GHz by a high concentration of surface current dispersion.

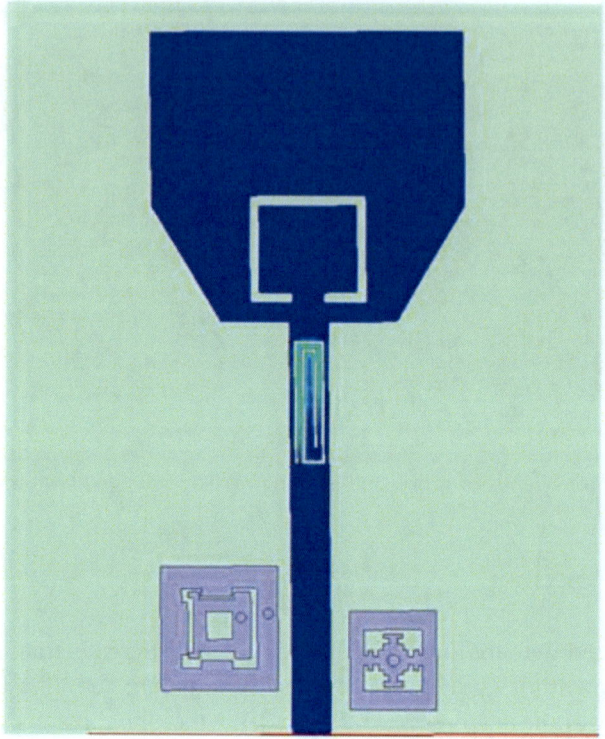

Figure 14. Surface Current Distribution.

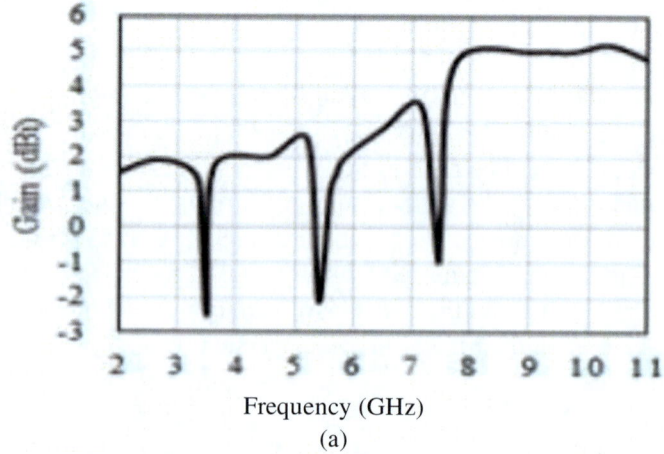

(a)

Figure 15. Gain of proposed antenna with EBG.

Gain

A directional antenna's gain is measured in comparison to an isotropic antenna. The intensity of the directional signal that an antenna transmits is specified by this standard. For the sake of accounting for potential losses, gains are more significant than directivity. In figure-15 shows the pass band gain of the antenna at notch frequency bands and in figure-17 shows the pass band gain of the antenna at 4.2 GHz is about 6 dB. Directivity is when an antenna's radiation pattern is focused in one direction, and efficiency makes up for antenna losses caused by flaws in the way it was made, problems with the surface coating, dielectric, resistance, VSWR, or other problems.

Return Loss

S11 is the reflection coefficient, representing the antenna's reflected power. If S11 is 0, the antenna reflects all power and emits none. S11 less than -10 dB means the gadget receives at least 90% of the input power and reflects less than 10% as shown in Figure 16.

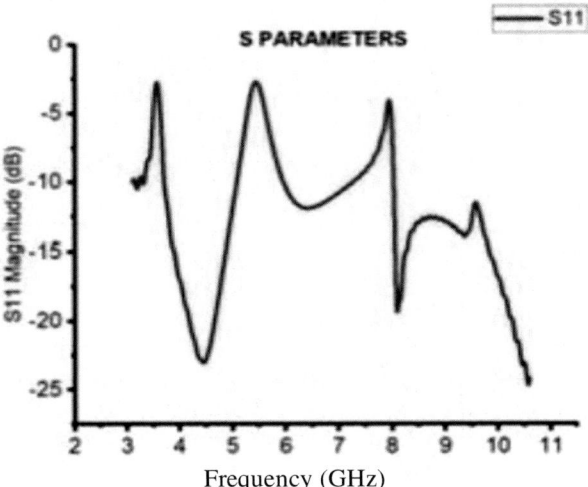

Figure 16. Return loss.

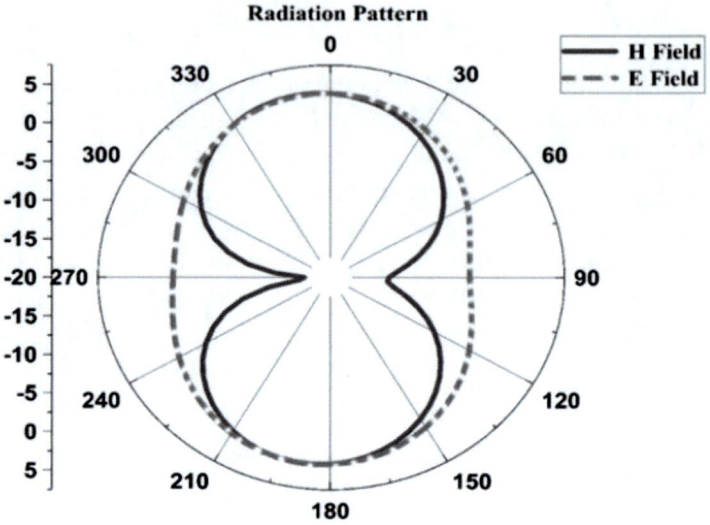

Figure 17. Radiation pattern.

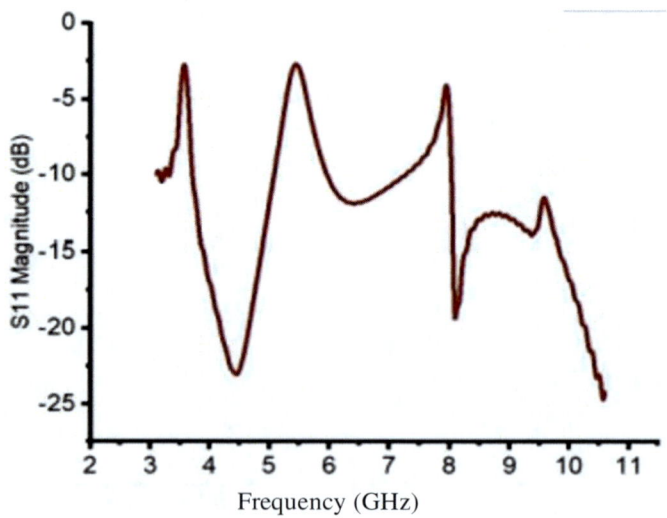

Figure 18(a). Measured Return loss.

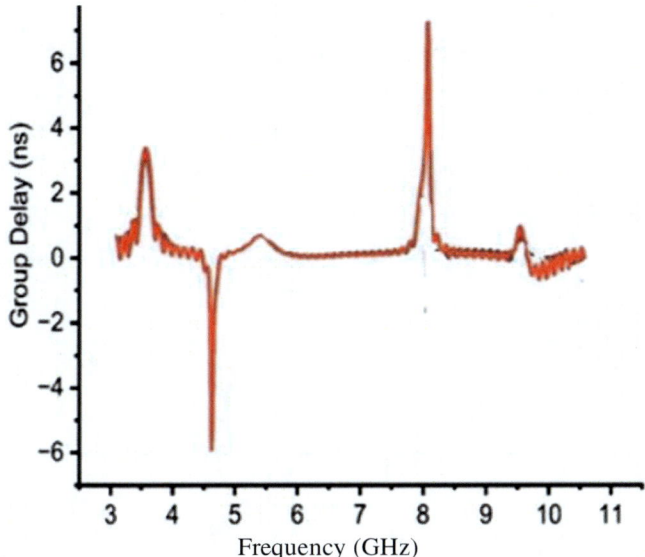

Figure 18(b). Measured Group delay.

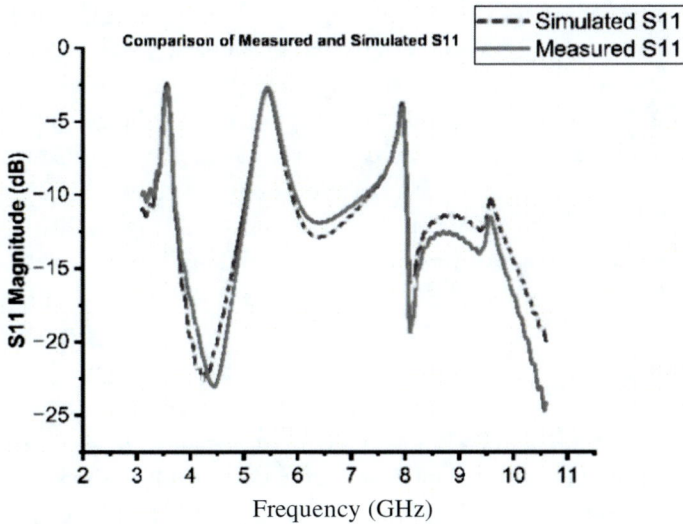

Figure 18(c). Comparison of Measured and Simulated S11 parameters.

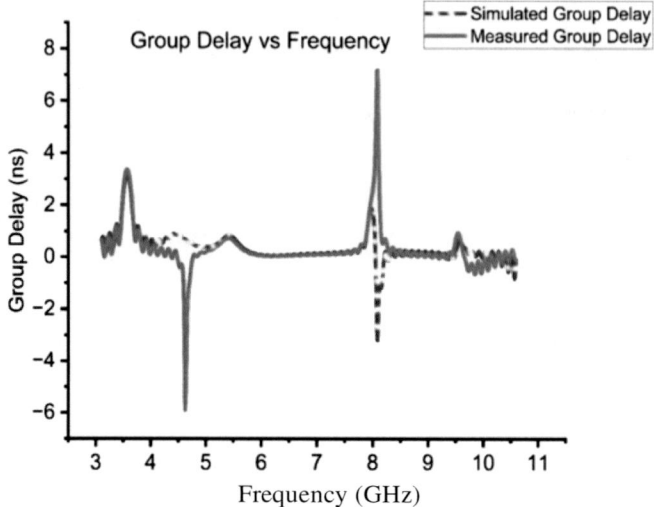

Figure 18(d). Comparison of Measured and Simulated group delay.

The Ultra Wide Band EBG based antenna is designed, the same has been fabricated and the simulated & measured results of the antenna are presented in the Figure 18(a) to 18(d). The Figure 18(a) represents the S11 of the physical antenna and the notch bands of WIMAX, WLAN & Satellite Communication were presented at frequency bands of 3.3–4.0 GH), 5.1–5.8 GHz & 7.2–7.4 GHz respectively. The Figure 18(c) indicates the comparison of Rerun loss (S11) for simulated & fabricated antenna and its clearly shows that there was a best correlation between both the results. The figure 18(b) shows the group delay of the physical antenna and Figure 18(d) represents group delay comparison of both simulated and fabricated antenna.

Conclusion

In this paper, a compact UWB antenna with triple band notching like WIMAX, WLAN and Satellite Downlink Communication bands at 3.65 GHz (3.3–4.0 GHz), 5.45 GHz (5.1–5.8 GHz) and 7.5 GHz (7.2–7.4 GHz) using both Two Via Edge Located (TVEL) EBG and Fractal EBG structures was designed using HFSS tool, The simulated Antenna was fabricated using RT/duriod 5880 substrate and simulated & fabricated results were compared. The experimentally measured results have shown a satisfactory agreement and consistent with the simulated results. The developed antenna provides good S parameters and good radiation patterns in both E- and H-planes over UWB range except in the notched band.

References

Babu, P. R. and R. K. Dasari, *Electromagnetic Band Gap based compact UWB Antenna with Dual Band Notch Response*.

Babu, P. R., D. Ramakrishna, and G. Ensermu, Triple Band-Notch UWB Antenna Embedded with Slot and EBG Structures. *Wireless Communications and Mobile Computing*, 2023. 2023.

Hammache, B., A. Messai, I. Messaoudene, T. A. Denidni, A compact ultra-wideband antenna with three C-shaped slots for notched band characteristics. *Microwave and Optical Technology Letters*, 2019. 61(1): p. 275-279.

Ibrahim, A. A., M. A. Abdalla, and A. Boutejdar, A printed compact band-notched antenna using octagonal radiating patch and meander slot technique for UWB applications. *Progress In Electromagnetics Research* M, 2017. 54: p. 153-162.

Jaglan, N., B. K. Kanaujia, S. D. Gupta, S. Srivastava, Design and development of an efficient EBG structures based band notched UWB circular monopole antenna. *Wireless Personal Communications*, 2017. 96: p. 5757-5783.

Jaglan, N., S. D. Gupta, B. K. Kanaujia, S. Srivastava., Band notched UWB circular monopole antenna with inductance enhanced modified mushroom EBG structures. *Wireless Networks*, 2018. 24: p. 383-393.

Mansouri, Z., Afsaneh Saee Arezoomand, Samaneh Heydari, Ferdows B. Zarrabi, Dual notch UWB fork monopole antenna with CRLH metamaterial load. *Progress In Electromagnetics Research* C, 2016. 65: p. 111-119.

Premalatha, B., G. Srikanth; P. Raveendra Babu; Mahesh V. Sonth, Design and analysis of two dimensional electromagnetic band gap antenna for WIFI applications. in *AIP Conference Proceedings*. 2021. AIP Publishing.

Premalatha, B., M. Prasad, and M. Murthy, A Novel Dual-Band Notched Hexagonal Monopole Antenna for UWB Applications. *International Journal of Simulation--Systems, Science & Technology*, 2018. 19(6).

Premalatha, B., M. Prasad, and M. Murthy, Multi-band notched antennas for UWB applications. *Radioelectronics and Communications Systems*, 2019. 62: p. 609-618.

Premalatha, B., M. V. Prasad, and M. B. Murthy, Compact penta band notched antenna using concentric rings with splitter bricks for ultra wide band applications. *Journal of Communications Technology and Electronics*, 2018. 63: p. 1379-1385.

Premalatha, B., P. R. Babu, and G. Srikanth, Compact fifth iteration fractal antenna for UWB applications. *Radioelectronics and Communications Systems*, 2021. 64: p. 325-329.

Rehman, S. ur and M. A. Alkanhal, Design and system characterization of ultra-wideband antennas with multiple band-rejection. *IEEE Access*, 2017. 5: p. 17988-17996.

Shaik, Latheef A. Chinmoy Saha, Jawad Y. Siddiqui, Yahia M. M. Antar., Ultra-wideband monopole antenna for multiband and wideband frequency notch and narrowband applications. *IET Microwaves, Antennas & Propagation*, 2016. 10(11): p. 1204-1211.

Singh, P., A., R. Khanna, and H. Singh, UWB antenna with dual notched band for WiMAX and WLAN applications. *Microwave and optical technology letters*, 2017. 59(4): p. 792-797.

Srivastava, K., Ashwani Kumar, Binod K. Kanaujia, Santanu Dwari, Anand Kumar Verma, Karu P. Esselle, Raj Mittra., Integrated GSM-UWB Fibonacci-type antennas with single, dual, and triple notched bands. *IET Microwaves, Antennas & Propagation*, 2018. 12(6): p. 1004-1012.

Vendik, I. B., Alexander Rusakov, Komsan Kanjanasit, Jiasheng Hong, Dmitry Filonov, " Ultrawideband (UWB) planar antenna with single, dual and triple-band notched characteristic based on electric ring resonator." *IEEE Antennas and wireless propagation letters*, 2017. 16: p. 1597-1600.

Washington, D., First report and order revision of Part 15 of the commission's rule regarding ultra-wideband transmission system FCC 02-48. *Federal Communications Commission*, 2002.

Yadav, A., M. D. Sharma, and R. P. Yadav, A CPW-fed CSRR and inverted U slot loaded triple band notched UWB antenna. *Progress In Electromagnetics Research* C, 2019. 89: p. 221-231.

Yang, F. and Y. Rahmat-Samii, Microstrip antennas integrated with electromagnetic band-gap (EBG) structures: A low mutual coupling design for array applications. *IEEE transactions on antennas and propagation*, 2003. 51(10): p. 2936-2946.

Yazdi, M. and N. Komjani, Design of a band-notched UWB monopole antenna by means of an EBG structure. *IEEE Antennas and Wireless Propagation Letters*, 2011. 10: p. 170-173.

Chapter 10

Hand Gesture Recognition Using a Deep Learning Model

J. Avanija[1]
Thoutireddy Shilpa[2]
Chikati Madhava Rao[3]
Nagendar Yamsani[4]
and K. Srujan Raju[5]

[1]Professor, School of Computing, Mohan Babu University, Tirupati, Andhra Pradesh, India.
[2]Assistant Professor, B V Raju Institute of Technology, Narsapur, Medak, Telangana. India.
[3]Assistant Professor, Department of CSE, CMR Technical Campus, Hyderabad, Telangana, India
[4]Assistant Professor, School of Computer Science and Artificial Intelligence, SR University, Warangal, India
[5]Professor, Department of CSE, CMR Technical Campus, Hyderabad, Telangana, India

Abstract

Artificial neural networks called convolutional neural networks are modeled after visual cortex. CNN will be used to perform conversion of image to a value-matrix given to certain values than to others. As a output of this process, every neuron present in the layer is connected to a minimal portion of the layer that was available previously, without taking into account all of the neurons that are present in the fully connected network. To begin with, image samples collected so that gaussian blur and a threshold could be applied to them. The Image data generator function in Keras is used to perform image augmentation. Each image in the batch is subjected to a series of arbitrary translations, rotations, and

In: Information and Knowledge Systems
Editors: Manaswini Pradhan and Satchidananda Dehurl
ISBN: 979-8-89113-303-7
© 2024 Nova Science Publishers, Inc.

other adjustments by ImageDataGenerator. In the proposed system, image features are extracted using the CNN algorithm.

Keywords: convolutional neural networks, hand gesture recognition, computer vision, deep learning

Introduction

Direct input from the hands can result in natural interaction. Hand gesture recognition is now considered to be one of the most crucial factors. The proposed system was developed to enhance existing technologies after taking into account contemporary world innovations like voice assistants, chat boxes, and other similar devices. This technique can be used to find a suitable dataset for controlling a video player with hand gestures. Find the most effective deep learning algorithm for recognising hand gestures and carrying out related operations. Hand gesture recognition is now one of the crucial elements. One of its many uses is touch-free control in public spaces like vending machines. It is employed in augmented reality to enhance sign language understanding and human-computer interaction.

Literature Review

A systematic literature review had been provided considering the work involving the recognition of hand gestures using machine learning algorithms. The authors also discussed the learning type used and the performance metrics to evaluate the method used. The survey was represented as three phases consisting of review planning, conducting review and reporting phase. The articles related to hand gesture recognition published in IEEE Xplore, Springer journals, ACM digital library, Wiley and Science direct were considered for survey (Abhishek, B et al., 2020). Computer Vision technique was used to predict the gestures made by hand considering the static and dynamic gestures. The method proposed initially recognizes the shape of the hand and traces the hand detected converting data for prediction. For recognition deep learning model with CNN based classification trained using the transfer learning method. The VGG16 architecture was used to train the model to predict hand gestures. The accuracy of proposed model is around 92% (Bhushan et al., 2022). Deep learning model was used to accurately predict the hand gestures using sign language. The proposed model used to predict the maximum gestures with sign language providing better accuracy compared to the existing techniques. Augmented data had been used to test the model. Initial phase of the proposed model acquires the captured image from camera and performs crop operation to extract the sign gestures and then model was trained through GCNN architecture using softmax classifier. The proposed model had given better results for many classes (Chung et al., 2019).

Human gestures can be recognized using appropriate mathematical algorithms in order to enable human computer interaction. The proposed work helps users to swich over the tasks such as scrolling of pages and swithchover between pages by training through machine learning model. The work was carried out as three phases involving human computer interaction through learning, detection and recognition. The proposed work identifies the gestures through 3D CNN-based deep learning model by capturing the images live through a web camera. The libraries such as OpenCV and Tensorflow were used for developing the proposed system (Cormoş et al., 2022; Sunitha Gurram et al., 2022). The authors (Ertam and Galip Aydın, 2017) applied different neural models over marcel dataset to identify hand gestures. The results obtained through different state of art models were compared through various performance metrics. Results revealed that the gesture recognition based on GoogleNet provided better results than other models. Machine learning algorithms such as Support Vector Machine, KNN, Naïve Byes, stochastic gradient descent, XGBoost and Logistic regression were used to classify the hand gestures. The dataset used to test the models was MNIST (Hasan, et al., 2017; Prabhakar et al., 2021). Gaussian and thresholding techniques were applied to the segmentation of the hand image. The direction of the hand gesture is identified using data from figure 1 and related to statistical variables like variance and covariance using the "Direction Analysis" method for calculating the slope of the object ((Hasan, et al., 2010).

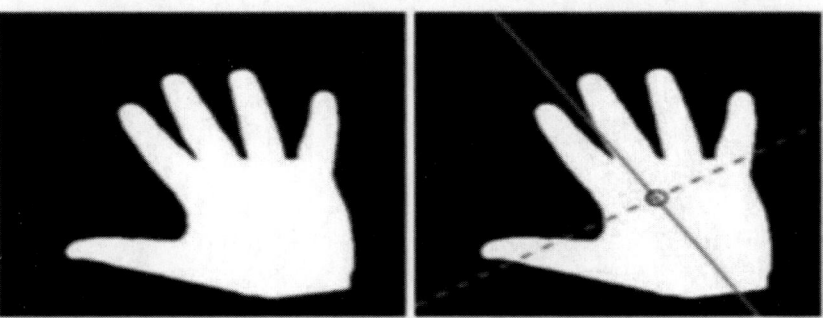

Figure 1. Computing the direction of hand.

Following segmentation, the image is subjected to the Gaussian distinction, used to consider direction of the hand. The image after segmentation was given a Gaussian distribution (Hasan and Pramod K. Mishra, 2010). After using the "gaussian function," the image was segregated as circular regions, according to the results, (Hussain et al., 2017). A total of "11 terraces" with a combined width of 0.1 (Hussain et al., 2017; Sharma and Sukhwinder Singh, 2021) are used to divide the shape. Nine terraces are created by dividing the width by 0.1: (1-0.9, 0.9-0.8", 0.8-0.7, 0.7-0.6", 0.6, 0.5,0.5-0.4", "0.3-0.2", "0.2-0.1"), the next terrace having a value less than 0.1, and the remaining terraces are for the external area that extends beyond the outer terrace (Hussain et al., 2017). In figure 2, the representation of the divisions is specified as graph.

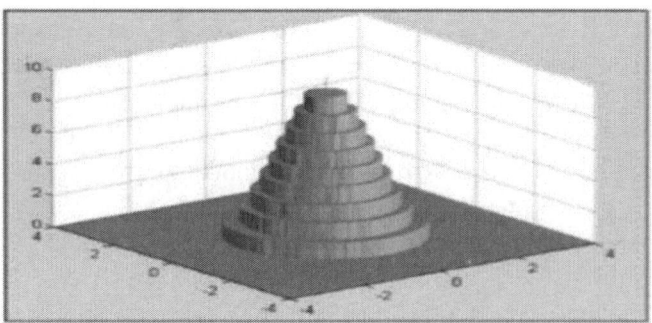

Figure 2. Terraces division considering value 0.1 as likelihood.

After preparing the hand's final shape through fitting, the Gaussian shape is matched with segmented image of hand used to extract the required features. Figure 3a and figure 3b shows the process in detail.

Figure 3a. "Terrace area" representation as Gaussian.

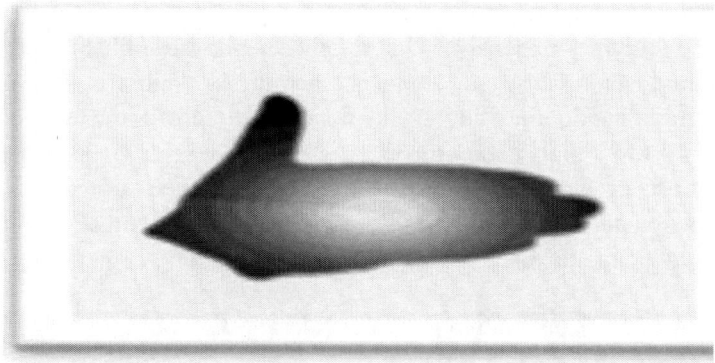

Figure 3b. Hand Image.

Any image after applying segmentation is normalised through trimming, then establishing centre mass of the image, and related coordinates adjusted to based on the centroid of object specified as hand at "X" and "Y" axis (Sharma and Sukhwinder Singh, 2021; Strezoski et al., 2018) The images of varing sizes generated depends on the object's centre of mass. See figure 4 in (Sharma and Sukhwinder Singh, 2021). By capturing live hand gestures using web camera, machine learning and deep learning models can more accurately predict hand gestures in both static and dynamic modes (Sun et al., 2018; Reshma et al., 2022).

Figure 4. Trimming process and Scaling normalization applied to input image.

Methodology

A hand gesture approach using instrumented gloves: Gloves with built-in sensors can record hand position and movement. Additionally, they can generate the precise directions of the palm and finger areas through sensors embedded in the gloves. However, this method limits client-PC collaboration because it necessitates a genuine connection between the two. Furthermore, these devices are very expensive. On the other hand, the sophisticated glove-based method makes use of contact innovation, which is regarded as Industrial-grade haptic innovation. The glove uses microfluidic technology to provide haptic input that enables the user to feel the weight, shape, and surface of a virtual object. The drawbacks of the glove approach shown in figure 5 are: The cost of data gloves is due to the sensor hub. For the client, wearing the glove every time for hand recognition becomes poorly organised.

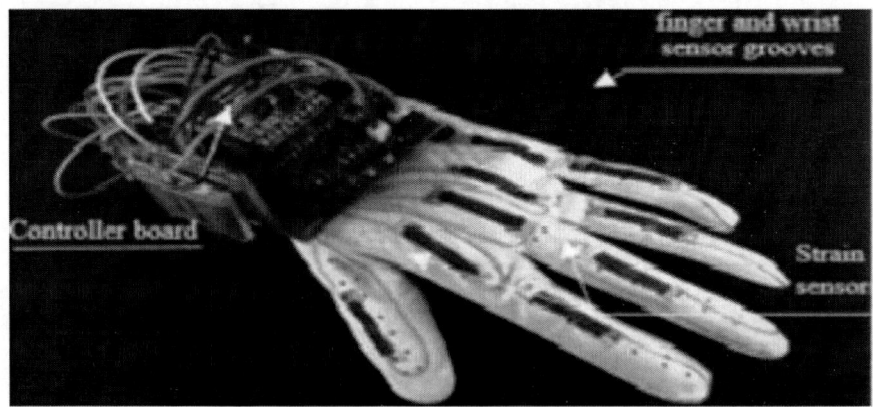

Figure 5. Sensor-based data glove.

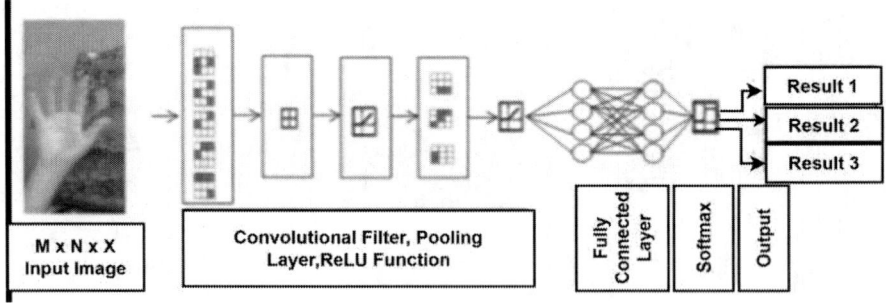

Figure 6. Proposed Model for Hand Gesture Recognition.

A method to identify hand motions using computer vision. The method used a camera vision-based sensor because it was a practical way to provide a contactless means of communication between people and computers. One can use camera types like "monocular," "fisheye," "TOF," and "IR." This method has problems with foundation, background complexity, event handling time in

Hand Gesture Recognition Using a Deep Learning Model 153

comparison to frame rate, foundational pictures, and closer views that appear to be hands with the same skin tone. This approach has problems with complexity brought on by escalating calculations and a lack of a precise ongoing framework for this cycle.

Deep-Learning Based Model: The biggest issue with this approach is the size of the dataset needed to familiarise the algorithm, which may affect how quickly it processes data. To order hand motions, "deep convolutional neural networks" is another technique. In this method, the resized image is given to the neural network without first going through the stages of division and recognition. One of the main categories of neural networks used for image recognition and characterization are "convolutional neural networks." CNNs are frequently used in fields like "face recognition," "object detection," etc. Before classifying an image, the CNN-based system takes it into consideration and processes it. Then consider "h x w x d" in terms of picture resolution specifying the height, width and dimension. Consider a "4 x 4 x 1" image of grayscale image and a "6 x 6 x 3" cluster of "RGB" network image, for example the RGB values specified as 3. As shown in figure 6, each image is put through the layered architecture specified as the "convolution," "pooling" and then "Softmax" function which is then applied in categorising an object with probabilistic values ranging betwwen 0 to 1 in order to prepare test the model consisting of layered architecture. Figure 7 below shows how CNN handles an image in its entirety, classifying objects according to values.

- An image matrix (volume) of dimension **(h x w x d)**
- A filter **(f_h x f_w x d)**
- Outputs a volume dimension **(h - f_h + 1) x (w - f_w + 1) x 1**

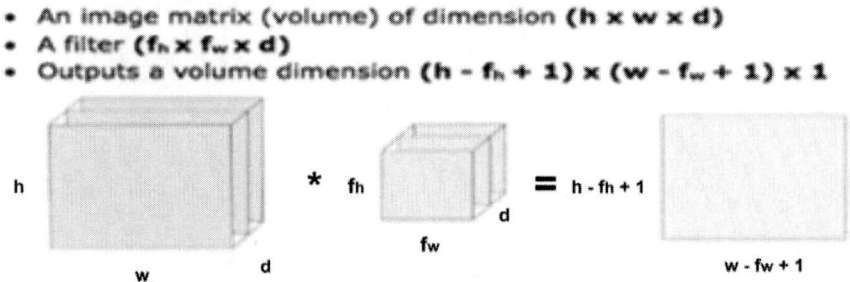

Figure 7. Image matrix multiplying the kernel.

The first layer that is used to extract features from an image is called "convolution." An image matrix and a filter are the inputs needed for this logical operation. Think about the 5 x 5 in figure 7 with a 3 x 3 filter matrix and image pixels with values of 0 and 1. The "Feature Map" output in figure

8 is the result obtained after the multiplication of the 3 x 3 filter matrix with the convolution of the 5 x 5 image matrix.

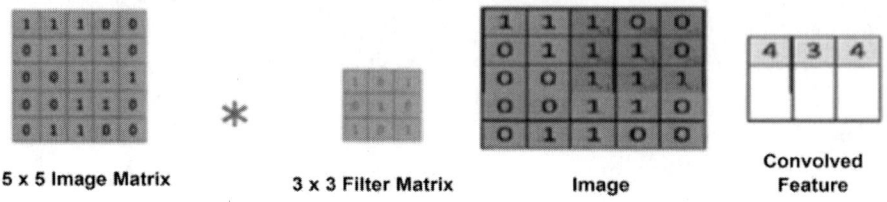

5 x 5 Image Matrix   3 x 3 Filter Matrix   Image   Convolved Feature

Figure 8. 3 x 3 Output matrix.

Operation	Filter	Convolved Image
Identity	$\begin{bmatrix} 0 & 0 & 0 \\ 0 & 1 & 0 \\ 0 & 0 & 0 \end{bmatrix}$	
	$\begin{bmatrix} 1 & 0 & -1 \\ 0 & 0 & 0 \\ -1 & 0 & 1 \end{bmatrix}$	
Edge Detection	$\begin{bmatrix} 0 & 1 & 0 \\ 1 & -4 & 1 \\ 0 & 1 & 0 \end{bmatrix}$	
	$\begin{bmatrix} -1 & -1 & -1 \\ -1 & 8 & -1 \\ -1 & -1 & -1 \end{bmatrix}$	
Sharpen	$\begin{bmatrix} 0 & -1 & 0 \\ -1 & 5 & -1 \\ 0 & -1 & 0 \end{bmatrix}$	
Box Blur (normalized)	$\frac{1}{9}\begin{bmatrix} 1 & 1 & 1 \\ 1 & 1 & 1 \\ 1 & 1 & 1 \end{bmatrix}$	
Gaussian Blur (Approximation)	$\frac{1}{16}\begin{bmatrix} 1 & 2 & 1 \\ 2 & 4 & 2 \\ 1 & 2 & 1 \end{bmatrix}$	

Figure 9. Different Filters.

By applying filters to an image, operations like "edge detection," "blur," and "sharpening" can be carried out on it. The examples below display photos with various filters applied, similar to figure 10. Rectified Linear Unit is referred to as a "ReLU" in a non-linear operation. The conclusion is (x) = max

(0,x). The purpose of ReLU is to add non-linearity to our "ConvNet." As a result of the fact that we want our "ConvNet" to learn non-negative linear values from empirical data. Other nonlinear functions, like tanh or sigmoid, can be used in place of "ReLU." ReLU is used by most data scientists because it performs better than alternatives. If the images were too large, the parameters were reduced in the section on pooling layers. Each map's dimensionality is decreased through spatial pooling, also referred to as subsampling or downsampling. The total of all feature map components is sum pooling. The matrix was converted into a vector and fed into a fully connected layer resembling a neural network. Figure 9 represents the operations of different filters and their convolved images.

Algorithm

- *Step 1:* First, import all the necessary machine learning libraries in python
- *Step 2:* Reading the data: Specify the location of dataset and perform read operation using list and convert into array.
- *Step 3:* Data Preprocessing: Scale the array by dividing it by 255 and reshape the Numpy array.
- *Step 4:* Data Splitting: Using train test split, divide data for training, testing and validation.
- *Step 5:* Model Building:Build the model using layers Conv,Maxpooling and dense.
- *Step 6:* Model Fitting:Compile the model first by specifying the required Hyper parameters, such as the optimizer, loss function, and metrics, before fitting the model. Here, our loss function is categorical crossentropy, and our optimization method is rmsprop. We have specified accuracy in metrics.
- *Step 7:* Evaluation: The Y test dataset should be used to compare the results of the X test dataset, and the accuracy value will be printed last.

Results and Discussions

Before beginning the neural network training, the input images were processed. After applying operations to the images to reduce noise, such as "resize," "threshold," "floodfill," and "Gaussian blur," the images were resized to "128x128" to ensure that all of the images were the same size. The threshold is then applied, with a value of 80 being the threshold after this step. Following this conversion to greyscale, the images are then binary. The pixel value is then compared to the threshold; if it is less than the threshold, the value is set to 0, otherwise it is 255. The hand's interior shadow-caused black areas will be filled to act as the connected region. The "floodfill" function from the "OpenCV" library will be used to fill the holes present inside the hand. The "bitwisenot" operation is used to flip the image. By applying the "ORoperation" to the thresholded output image as shown in figure 10, the inverted image generated can be used in the region.

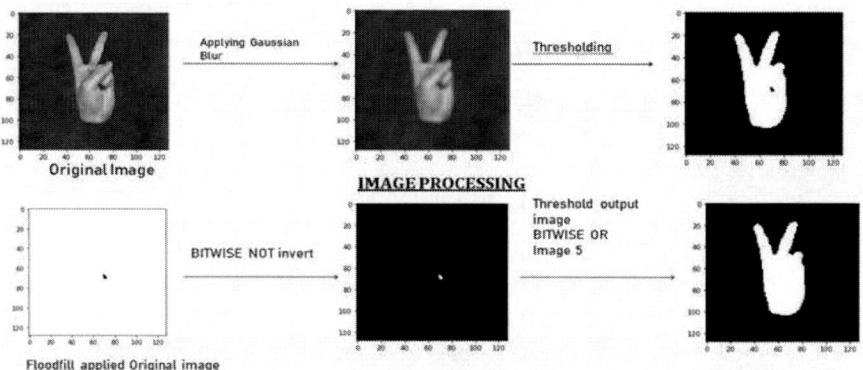

Figure 10. Image processing.

To implement the image augmentation shown in Figure 11, the Imagedatagenerator function of Keras is used. Each image in the batch is subjected to a series of arbitrary translations, rotations, and other effects by ImageDataGenerator. An approach called "image data augmentation" produces "transformed," "translated," and "image manipulation" versions of training dataset images that are in the same class as the original image, such as shifts, flips, and zooms. After verifying the images, we will feed them to the model, which will then use the training set to identify the gestures in the images. The results will be shown in a new window. The result of the gesture detection will be shown in a new window.

Hand Gesture Recognition Using a Deep Learning Model 157

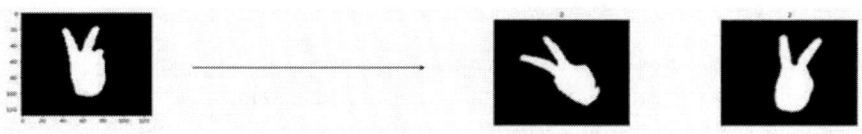

Figure 11. Image augmentation.

Table 1. Epoch accuracy of the proposed model

Epoch	Accuracy (%)
1	15.64
2	85.37
3	98.55
4	99.16
5	97.24

The model's accuracy is shown in Table 1 based on the training data and number of epochs. The model's accuracy is 98.16%. The outcomes based on the inputs shown in Figure 12.

Figure 12. Gesture Recognition using Proposed Model.

Conclusion

The proposed work used a convolution neural network to recognise hand gestures. The images were enhanced and processed to strengthen model training. The CNN will choose the images' best elements on its own. The accuracy of the CNN Algorithm when using stochastic gradient descent as the optimizer is good with a lower error rate. The outcomes are specific to this dataset and might not apply to other datasets. The images considered as input were with backgrounds in testing and training to eliminate the background, which will be helpful. The proposed system can be enhanced by concentrating on erasing the background from the input images. So we can make this proposed system work anywhere, regardless of background.

Disclaimer

None

References

Abhishek, B., Kanya Krishi, M. Meghana, Mohammed Daaniyaal, and H. S. Anupama. "Hand gesture recognition using machine learning algorithms." *Computer Science and Information Technologies* 1, no. 3 (2020): 116-120.

Bhushan, Shashi, Mohammed Alshehri, Ismail Keshta, Ashish Kumar Chakraverti, JitendraRajpurohit, and Ahed Abugabah. "An experimental analysis of various machine learning algorithms for hand gesture recognition." *Electronics* 11, no. 6 (2022): 968.

Chung, Hung-Yuan, Yao-Liang Chung, and Wei-Feng Tsai. "An efficient hand gesture recognition system based on deep CNN." In *2019 IEEE International Conference on Industrial Technology (ICIT)*, pp. 853-858. IEEE, 2019.

Cormoș, Angel Ciprian, Răzvan Andrei Gheorghiu, Valentin Alexandra STAN, and Ion Spirea Dănăilă. "Use of TensorFlow and OpenCV to detect vehicles." In *2020 12th International Conference on Electronics, Computers and Artificial Intelligence (ECAI)*, pp. 1-4. IEEE, 2020.

Ertam, Fatih, and Galip Aydın. "Data classification with deep learning using Tensorflow." In *2017 international conference on computer science and engineering (UBMK)*, pp. 755-758. IEEE, 2017.

Hasan, Mokhar M., and Pramod K. Mishra. "Features fitting using multivariate gaussian distribution for hand gesture recognition." *International Journal of Computer Science & Emerging Technologies IJCSET* 3, no. 2 (2012): 73-80.

Hasan, Mokhtar M., and Pramod K. Mishra. "Robust gesture recognition using gaussian distribution for features fitting." *International Journal of Machine Learning and Computing* 2, no. 3 (2012): 266.

Hasan, Mokhtar M., and Pramod K. Mishra. "HSV brightness factor matching for gesture recognition system." *International Journal of Image Processing (IJIP)* 4, no. 5 (2010): 456-467.

Hussain, Soeb, Rupal Saxena, Xie Han, Jameel Ahmed Khan, and Hyunchul Shin. "Hand gesture recognition using deep learning." In *2017 International SoC design conference (ISOCC)*, pp. 48-49. IEEE, 2017.

Oudah, Munir, Ali Al-Naji, and Javaan Chahl. "Hand gesture recognition based on computer vision: a review of techniques." *journal of Imaging* 6, no. 8 (2020): 73.

Prabhakar, Telagarapu, Gurram Sunitha, J. Avanija Gudavalli Madhavi, and K. Reddy Madhavi. "Automatic Detection of Diabetic Retinopathy in Retinal Images: A Study of Recent Advances." Annals of the Romanian Society for Cell Biology (2021): 15277-15289.

Reshma, G., Chiai Al-Atroshi, Vinay Kumar Nassa, B. T. Geetha, Gurram Sunitha, Mohammad Gouse Galety, and S. Neelakandan. "Deep Learning-Based Skin Lesion Diagnosis Model Using Dermoscopic Images." Intelligent Automation & Soft Computing 31, no. 1 (2022).

Strezoski, Gjorgji, Dario Stojanovski, Ivica Dimitrovski, and Gjorgji Madjarov. "Hand gesture recognition using deep convolutional neural networks." In *ICT Innovations 2016: Cognitive Functions and Next Generation ICT Systems*, pp. 49-58. Springer International Publishing, 2018.

Sun, Jing-Hao, Ting-Ting Ji, Shu-Bin Zhang, Jia-Kui Yang, and Guang-Rong Ji. "Research on the hand gesture recognition based on deep learning." In *2018 12th International symposium on antennas, propagation and EM theory (ISAPE)*, pp. 1-4. IEEE, 2018.

Sunitha, Gurram, K. Geetha, S. Neelakandan, Aditya Kumar Singh Pundir, S. Hemalatha, and Vinay Kumar. "Intelligent deep learning-based ethnicity recognition and classification using facial images." Image and Vision Computing 121 (2022): 104404.

Chapter 11

A Study on Blockchain-Cloud Hybrid Model-Based Healthcare Systems

**Swatisipra Das
and Minati Mishra**
Postgraduate Department of Computer Science, Fakir Mohan University,
Balasore, Odisha, India

Abstract

With the digitization of the healthcare systems, securely maintaining and sharing health records have become some of the crucial tasks. Before the introduction of cloud computing, digital healthcare systems were majorly represented by client/server models but when cloud computing came into market with its most attractive functionalities such as on-demand access and usage convenience, the healthcare system migrated to cloud based healthcare system. In spite of the myriad of opportunities provided by the cloud-based systems, these suffer from a major problem that is the dependency upon the third-party service providers and to avoid this dependency issue researchers have started proposing "Blockchain based systems." The Blockchain-Cloud combined model-based healthcare systems eliminate third party dependency, reduce the implementation cost and provide better scalability to handle the continuously growing health records. Several such hybrid models are proposed by numbers of researcher and in this chapter, we present a detailed study on these hybrid model-based healthcare systems as well as suggested a "An Accountable Cloud based Healthcare data Management system using Blockchain (ACHMBC)" that ensures accountability in addition to confidentiality, Integrity, authenticity and access control.

Keywords: Blockchain, Cloud, digital healthcare systems, Blockchain-cloud healthcare models

In: Information and Knowledge Systems
Editors: Manaswini Pradhan and Satchidananda Dehurl
ISBN: 979-8-89113-303-7
© 2024 Nova Science Publishers, Inc.

Introduction

The traditional healthcare system is like moving to the doctor's clinic, making an appointment, being diagnosed by a doctor, and according to the prescription taking medicine from a clinical store. The digital healthcare system says that no need to visit doctors all the time, you can monitor your health condition by using digital healthcare systems. It provides easy diagnosis, and easy storing of patients' medical reports, at a low cost, within minimal time and anywhere access at any time. Now the question will come - why researchers are moving towards Cloud based digital healthcare systems and then again why towards Blockchain based Cloud healthcare systems? The answers are discussed in the following subsections.

Why Cloud Based Digital Healthcare Systems?

In this era of information technology, people have started moving towards cloud to get hardware as well as software services on a pay-per-use basis. The major and interesting characteristics of the cloud are, location Independence, multi-tenancy, high reliability, high scalability, etc (Linthicum 2009, Grossman 2009, 23-27). The general architecture of the cloud is shown in "Figure 1" where the numbering starts with letter "O" represents the data upload procedure of owner and letter "U" represents the data access procedure of users. Now coming to the question of why researchers have collaborated cloud with healthcare systems? As the population of the world is growing so is the healthcare data hence, to store and maintain these rich amounts of data for several years, access the data in any time and anywhere are the major problems with traditional healthcare systems. All these problems can be solved by adopting the cloud in healthcare systems (Alzoubaidi 2016, 1-6, Singh et al., 2019, 930-933, Padhy et al., 2012, 149-157).

Why Blockchain Based Cloud Digital Healthcare Systems?

Blockchain technology is the solution to all security problems that arise through a single point of failure or central dependency. It is the technology based on the motto "No need to trust anybody." As, it is following the decentralization concept hence, for transaction verification and for keeping

A Study on Blockchain-Cloud Hybrid Model-Based Healthcare Systems   163

logs of transactions executed on the network, Blockchain uses Distributed Ledger technology (DLT) at the end of every participant. Consensus algorithms are used in Blockchain, through which all the participants reach a common decision which is best for the network. If the conditions were met then to execute some operations automatically, it uses smart contracts. It uses hash functions to achieve integrity of the data stored in a particular block and to link the block with other which is present just before it (Das et al., 2022, 1-6). The structure of block and Blockchain is shown in "Figure 2." A block is divided into two parts such as header and body. The header consists of Time Stamp (TS), Previous block Hash (PH), nonce and Merkle Root (MR - the combined hash of all the transactions stored in a particular block). Researchers have adopted Blockchain with cloud-based healthcare systems because the cloud-based healthcare systems suffer from security problems such as, single point of failure, dependency on a third party, malicious insider, access control etc. and the use of Blockchain can solve these issues easily.

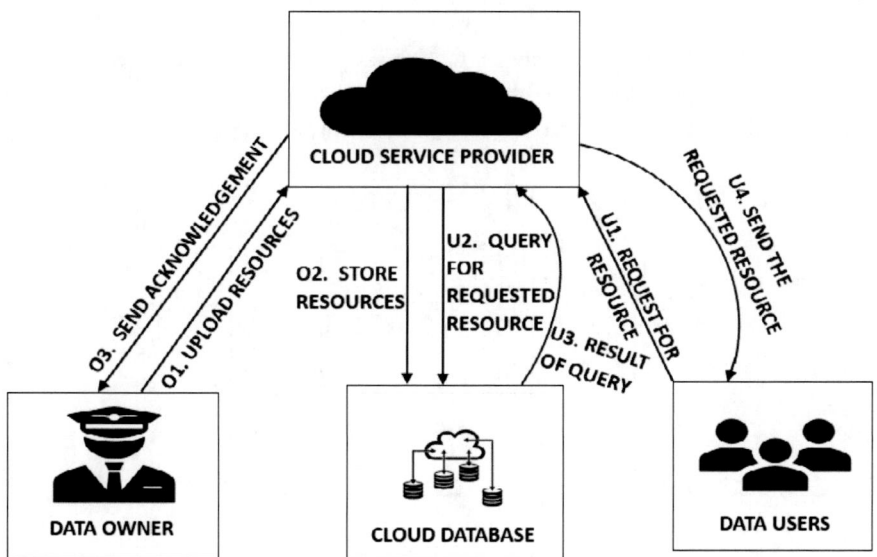

Figure 1. General Structure of Cloud.

Motivation

Among all the domains healthcare is the most important one and healthcare data is an important asset. To make available health diagnosis any time and any where, researchers started proposing digital healthcare systems which played a very important role at the time of covid-19 pandemic. People could perform their tests as well as they were getting diagnoses by doctors through these digital healthcare apps. To store and process the medical data efficiently researchers have started proposing cloud-based healthcare systems. Cloud has several attractive features such as on-demand self service, ubiquitous network access, location-independence, resource pooling, rapid elasticity and pay-per-use (Linthicum 2009). But, the main concern in this case is about the security of data. As medical data are highly confidential in nature, we can not trust on a third party. To achieve data security few researchers are focusing on decentralized Blockchain based technologies in cloud-based healthcare systems. An extensive research work has been seen in last few years to avoid different kinds of security issues those arise in cloud-based healthcare systems. This has motivated us to conduct a systematic survey on the Blockchain based cloud healthcare frameworks proposed to resolve some major kinds of security issues of cloud healthcare systems.

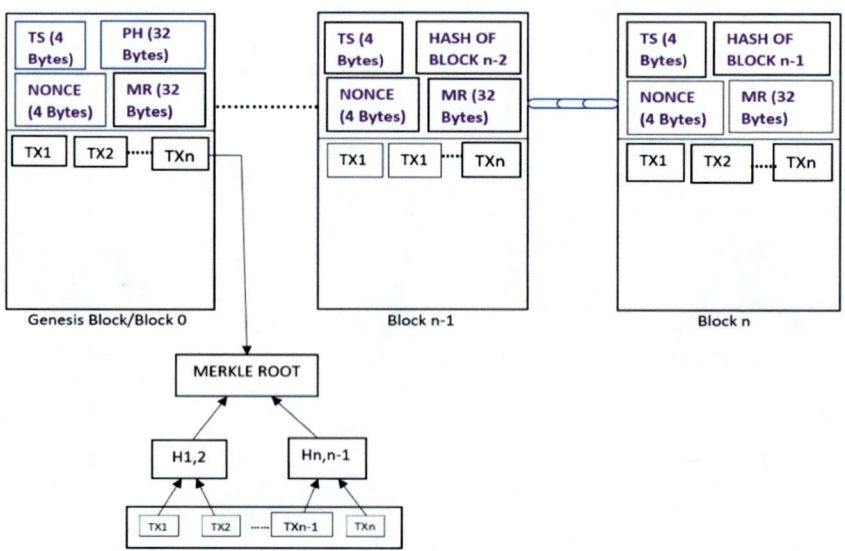

Figure 2. Structure of Blockchain.

A Study on Blockchain-Cloud Hybrid Model-Based Healthcare Systems   165

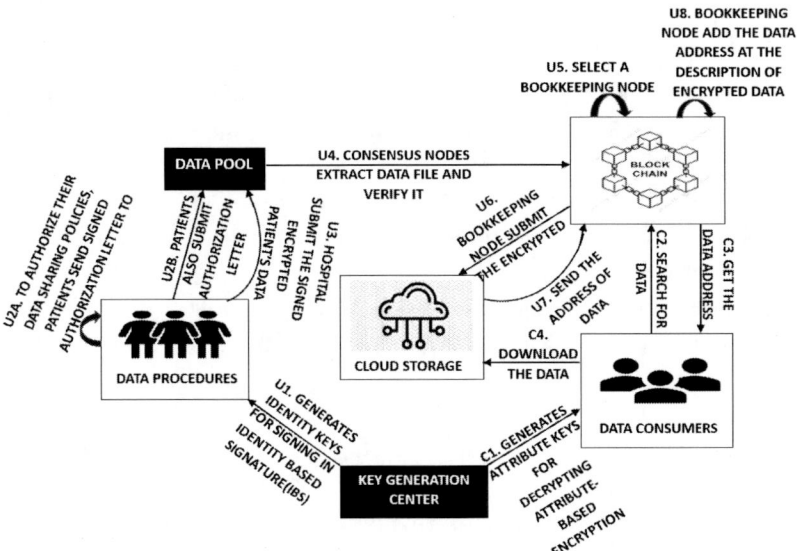

Figure 3. Data storage and access of Secure cloud-based EHR system using attribute-based encryption and blockchain.

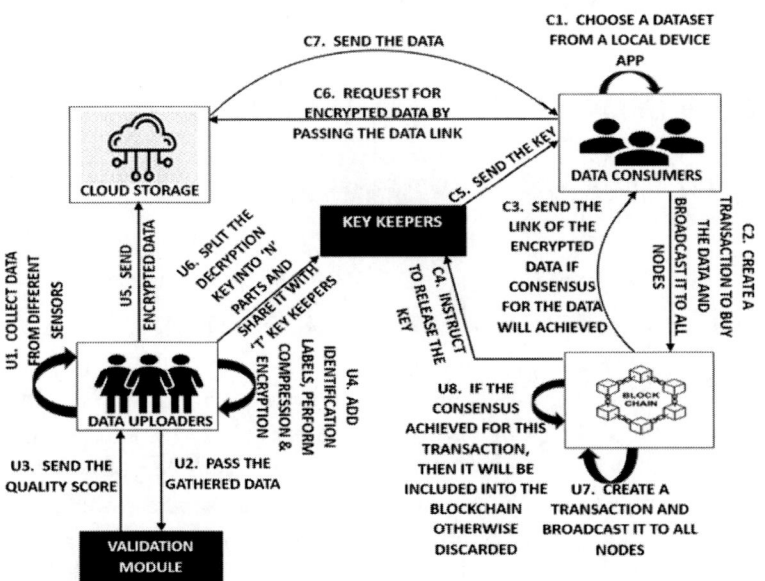

Figure 4. Data upload and access of Blockchain-based personal health data sharing system using Cloud storage.

Our Contributions

The aim of this paper is to conduct a comprehensive study on different Blockchain based cloud healthcare frameworks. Following are the major contributions of this paper:

1. An extensive study on the Blockchain based cloud healthcare frameworks.
2. Comparison of all the models from security point of view.
3. Some of the future research directions are discussed in section 4.

Research Questions

This paper intends to address the following research questions:

RQ1. What are the different Blockchain based cloud healthcare systems those are proposed along with their working?

RQ2. Which security parameters are focused on by the existing models to make them secure and their limitations if any?

Blockchain-Cloud Hybrid Model Based Healthcare Systems

In this section some of the Blockchain-based existing cloud healthcare systems are discussed in following subsections.

Secure Cloud-based Electronic Health Records (EHR) System

To achieve confidentiality, authentication and integrity of data in Cloud based EHR systems the authors of (Wang and Song 2018, 1-9) have proposed "Cloud based EHR systems using attribute-based cryptosystem and Blockchain." Different entities involved in this framework are data producers (hospitals, patients), data consumers (users, medical research centers), key generation center, data pool, Blockchain and cloud storage. To upload the data, patient first sends authorization letter to the hospital and the data pool. After that the hospital sends the encrypted signed data to the data pool. The consensus nodes of the Blockchain extract the data file from the pool for verification and select a bookkeeping(miner) node. The bookkeeping node submits the encrypted data to cloud and update the encrypted data file with its address location in cloud. To access data, the consumer searches for the data first in Blockchain, receives the data address from the Blockchain and downloads the data from cloud. The diagrammatic representation of the upload and access of this model is shown in "Figure 3." The data storage procedures are numbered by using the starting letter "U" and access procedure of consumers are numbered with initial letter "C."

Blockchain-based Personal Health Data Sharing System

To deal with continuous and dynamic health data the authors of (Zheng et al., 2018, 1-6) have proposed "Blockchain-based Personal Health Data Sharing System Using Cloud Storage." This model emphasises upon the security of the decryption key. After collection of data from different sensors the data uploader checks the quality of data and sends the encrypted data to the cloud. To keep the decryption key, secure the uploader splits it into "n" parts and sends the parts to "t" key keepers. The record of data upload is stored in the Blockchain in the form of transactions if consensus is achieved. For accessing data, the consumer first sends the request to Blockchain and if consensus is achieved, the link of encrypted data is sent to the consumer. The key keeper releases the decryption key to the requester using which the encrypted data is downloaded from the cloud. The complete data upload and sharing procedure is defined shown in "Figure 4" where the data upload procedures requested by data uploaders are marked with initial letter "U" and the access methods are represented with starting letter "C."

Secure Sharing Model

The Secure Sharing (SS) (Feng et al., 2019, 429-438) model based on Blockchain involves users, data owner, cloud server, Blockchain, first level medical node alliance (HL1), second level medical node alliance (HL2). In case of data storage, the data owner sends a storage request to the node "N0" in HL1. "N0" broadcasts the request to the entire network. The check node "C0" verifies the user identity and if it is verified then node "N0" encrypts the data and store it in its own database and also share the information with the entire network. If more than 1/3 nodes receive the information, user gets an acknowledgement from "N0." The workflow of data storage is shown in "Figure 5." In data sharing, the user sends the request to the node whose current value is "R," which broadcasts the message and sends the user identity verification request to check node "C1" of HL2. If it is verified and more than 1/3 nodes in HL1 receive the request message then "R" searches requested data block in Blockchain. After getting the block, "R" converts the information to user satisfiable form and sends the data to user. The workflow of data sharing is shown in "Figure 6."

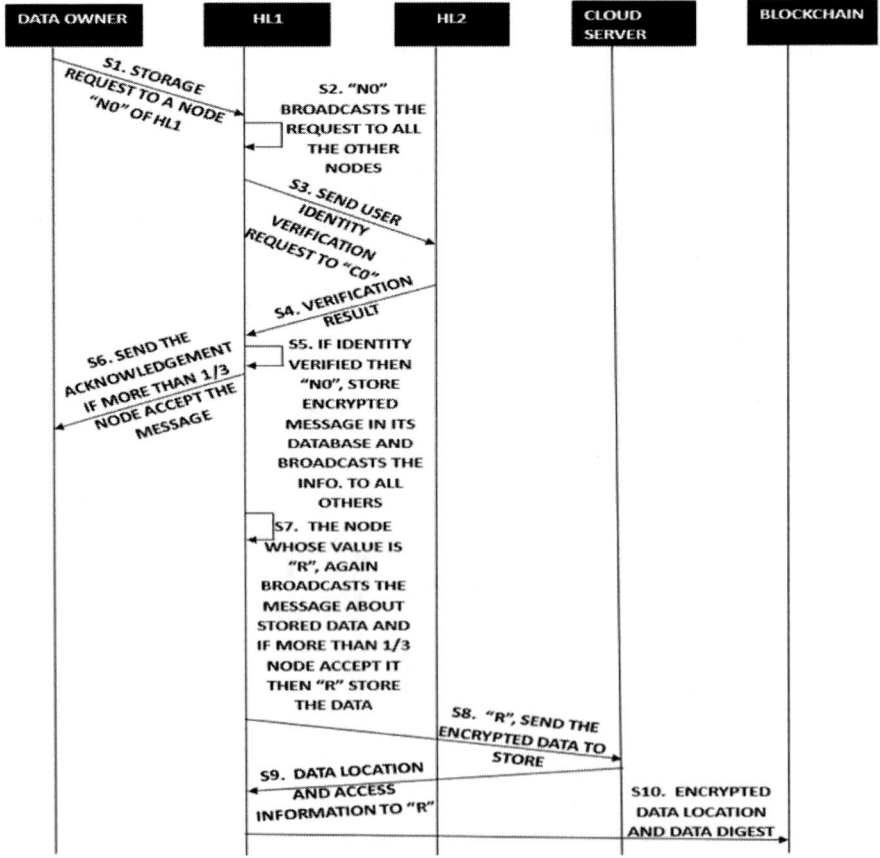

Figure 5. Data storage procedure of SS Model based on Blockchain in Medical cloud.

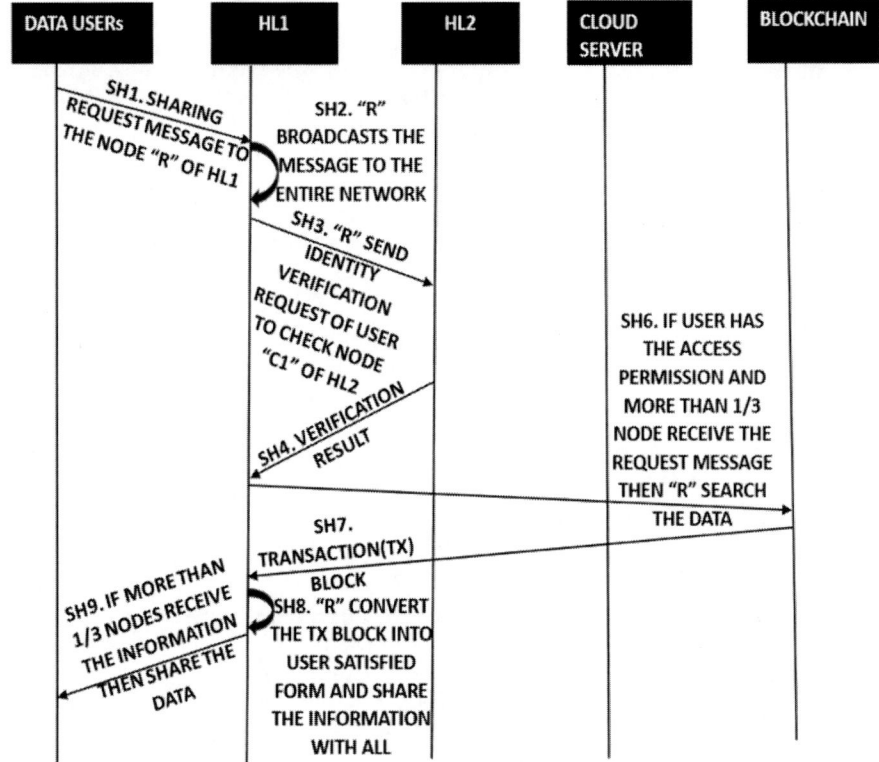

Figure 6. Data sharing procedure of SS Model based on Blockchain in Medical cloud.

Keyless Signature Infrastructure (KSI) and Elephant Herding Optimization- Opposition Based Learning (EHO-OBL) based e-health System

To provide better authentication, integrity and to reduce key generation time the author of (Verma 2022, 1-14) has proposed a KSI and EHO-OBL based model name as "Blockchain-based Privacy Preservation framework for healthcare data in cloud environment." This model is extended version of the model proposed in (Nagasubramanian 2020, 639-647). With the work of (Nagasubramanian 2020, 639-647) the author has added modified EHO with fitness-based computation and blowfish algorithm. Here as more improtance is given to reduce the key generation time for that author have added OBL with this modified EHO.

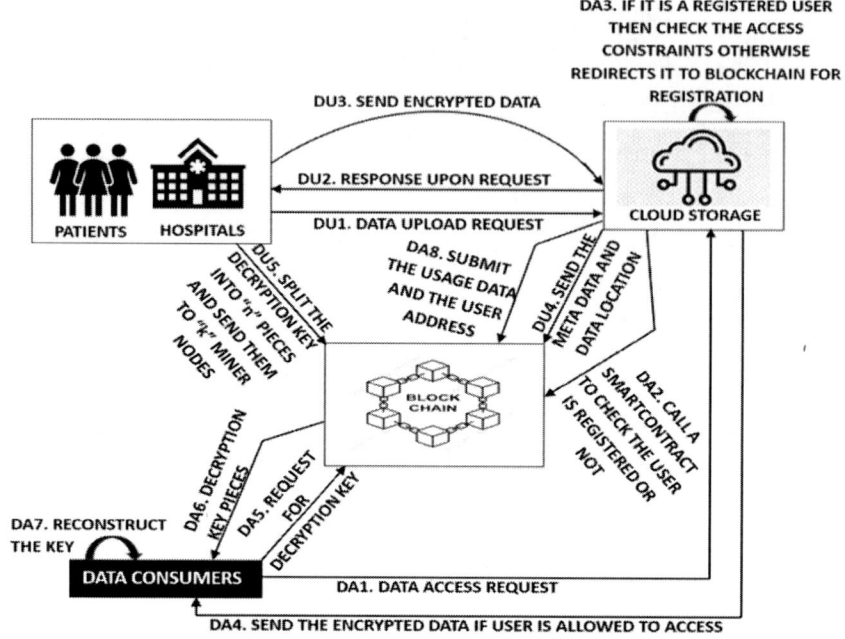

Figure 7. Data upload and access procedure of model "ACHMBC."

Integration of Healthcare 4.0 and Blockchain in Cloud based EHRs

The authors of (Mahajan 2022, 1-14) have proposed a model based on IoT, fog, cloud and Blockchain. Authors have described their model in the form of four layers such as: IoT, Fog, CSP and Blockchain layer. In IoT layer the data producers collect data from various sensors and store it locally in fog layer. After that cloud layer performs data stockpiling and the CSP sends the meta data and logs to Blockchain. But the detailed procedures of data storage, access and access log keeping is missing in this paper.

Proposed Model

In the above existing Blockchain-cloud based healthcare models, importance has been given on achieving confidentiality, integrity and authenticity on medical data uploading and sharing but, no method is proposed to track which user has accessed what? hence, in our proposed model "An Accountable Cloud based Healthcare data Management system using Blockchain (ACHMBC)" we have tried to take care of the data retrieval log. The model is described in "Figure 7," where the data uploading procedures are defined with starting letter "DU" and sharing procedures are with "DA." Data producers upload the encrypted data in cloud. Cloud to store the meta data along with location of this data in Blockchain. To keep the decryption key secure, producer will divide the decryption key into "n" pieces and submit them to "k" miner nodes of Blockchain. Whenever data access request comes to the cloud, it first checks whether the requested user is registered or not by calling a smart contract. If it a registered user then cloud will check the access constraints of this particular user otherwise cloud redirect the user to Blockchain for registration. After matching of access constraints of requested user, cloud sends the encrypted data. Then user sends request to Blockchain for decryption key. Now to keep the logs of a particular user's data usage, after each user session cloud will generate URL of user's data usage along with address of user and submit it to Blockchain.

Comparison of our model (ACHMBC) with the existing models from security perspectives

Comparison of our model with the existing models from Security perspectives healthcare is the most important domain so as to secure the medical data is a big challenge. On the basis of basic security factors such as confidentiality, integrity, authenticity, access control and accountability, the comparison of existing Blockchain-Cloud based healthcare model with our model is shown in "Table. 1." Where those factors are achieved by a particular model is represented by "Y" and those are not achieved by "N." In the model proposed in (Wang and Song 2018, 1-9), there is no procedure to achieve data accountability and the keys for data producers as well as consumers are generated by a third party Key Generation Center (KGC). The model proposed in (Zheng et al., 2018, 1-6), there is also no procedure to achieve accountability and here also the decryption key is stored in a third party entity. In paper (Feng et al., 2019, 429-438, Verma 2022, 1-14), the proposed model is also unable to achieve accountability.

Table 1. Comparison of Security factors achieved by existing blockchain-cloud healthcare systems with our proposed model

Author Name & Year	Confidentiality	Integrity	Authenticity	Access control	Accountability
Wang, Hao, et al., & 2018	Y	Y	Y	Y	N
Zheng, Xiaochen, et al., & 2018	Y	Y	Y	Y	N
Feng, Tao, et al., & 2019	Y	Y	Y	Y	N
Verma, Garima, et al., & 2022	Y	Y	Y	Y	N
Our model	Y	Y	Y	Y	Y

Future Research Directions

Although many researchers have proposed various Blockchain-based solutions to resolve the security issues coming in cloud e-heathcare systems but still there are huge research gaps. The future research directions are listed below.
1. Implementation of our proposed model.
2. Reduction of the medical data access time consumption in our model.

Conclusion

Cloud and Blockchain are the two famous terms for toady's IT users. To maintain the rich amount of medical data for long term, access of data in any time and in location independent manner, few researchers have proposed cloud based healthcare systems. But there is some security issues with cloud based healthcare systems and for that we need decentralized, distributed cloud based healthcare system. Blockchain is the most famous decentralized, distributed system so, researchers have started proposing Blockchain-Cloud based healthcare systems. A review on Blockchain-based healthcare systems is carried out in this paper. By looking the security leakage of some existing models, we have proposed one model named as "ACHMBC." In section 4 a security comparison among the existing models and our model is there and in section 5 some of the future directions are listed. The uniqueness and findings of this paper are listed below.

1. The research gaps in some of Blockchain-Cloud based healthcare models.
2. Proposal of an ACHMBC model.
3. Comparison of security factors achieved by some Blockchain-Cloud hybrid model based healthcare systems with ACHMBC model.

References

Alzoubaidi, Abdel Rahman. "Cloud computing national e-health services: data center solution architecture." *International Journal of Computer Science and Network Security (IJCSNS) 16*, no. 9 (2016): 1.

Das, Swatisipra, Jayanti Rout, and Minati Mishra. "Blockchain Technology: Applications and Open Issues." In *2022 International Conference on Communication, Computing and Internet of Things (IC3IoT)*, pp. 1-6. IEEE, 2022.

Feng, Tao, Ying Jiao, and Junli Fang. "Secure Sharing Model Based on Block Chain in Medical Cloud (Short Paper)." In *Collaborative Computing: Networking, Applications and Worksharing: 15th EAI International Conference, CollaborateCom 2019, London, UK, August 19-22, 2019, Proceedings 15*, pp. 429-438. Springer International Publishing, 2019.

Grossman, Robert L. "The case for cloud computing." *IT professional 11*, no. 2 (2009): 23-27.

Linthicum, David S. Cloud computing and SOA convergence in your enterprise: a step-by-step guide. *Pearson Education*, 2009.

Mahajan, Hemant B., Ameer Sardar Rashid, Aparna A. Junnarkar, Nilesh Uke, Sarita D. Deshpande, Pravin R. Futane, Ahmed Alkhayyat, and Bilal Alhayani. "Integration of Healthcare 4.0 and blockchain into secure cloud-based electronic health records systems." *Applied Nanoscience* (2022): 1-14.

Nagasubramanian, Gayathri, Rakesh Kumar Sakthivel, Rizwan Patan, Amir H. Gandomi, Muthuramalingam Sankayya, and Balamurugan Balusamy. "Securing e-health records using keyless signature infrastructure blockchain technology in the cloud." Neural Computing and *Applications* 32 (2020): 639-647.

Padhy, Rabi Prasad, Manas Ranjan Patra, and Suresh Chandra Satapathy. "Design and implementation of a cloud based rural healthcare information system model." *Univers J Appl Comput Sci Technol 2*, no. 1 (2012): 149-157.

Singh, Inderpreet, Deepak Kumar, and Sunil Kumar Khatri. "Improving the efficiency of e-healthcare system based on cloud." In *2019 Amity International Conference on Artificial Intelligence (AICAI), pp. 930-933*. IEEE, 2019.

Verma, Garima. "Blockchain-based privacy preservation framework for healthcare data in cloud environment." *Journal of Experimental & Theoretical Artificial Intelligence* (2022): 1-14.

Wang, Hao, and Yujiao Song. "Secure cloud-based EHR system using attribute-based cryptosystem and blockchain." *Journal of medical systems* 42, no. 8 (2018): 152.

Zheng, Xiaochen, Raghava Rao Mukkamala, Ravi Vatrapu, and Joaqun Ordieres-Mere. "Blockchain-based personal health data sharing system using cloud storage." In *2018 IEEE 20th international conference on e-health networking, applications and services (Healthcom)*, pp. 1-6. IEEE, 2018.

About the Editors

Dr. Manaswini Pradhan received B.E. in Computer Science and Engineering, M.Tech. in Computer Science from Utkal University, Odisha, India, and Ph.D. degree in the field of Information and Communication Technology from Fakir Mohan University, Odisha. Currently she is working as an Assistant Professor in P.G. Department of Information and Communication Technology, Fakir Mohan University, Orissa, India. She has been in the teaching profession for the last eighteen years, and during this period she also has acquired research experience in Artificial Neural Network, Data mining, Bioinformatics and other topics in the broad subject of Information & Communication Technology. She has been awarded research projects by Department of Science & Technology, Govt. of India, and UGC, New Delhi. She has published research papers in national & international journals, a book chapter published by *Taylor & Francis*, *Springer*, *IBI Global*, *Springer* and presented papers in various conferences. She is involved in guiding M.Tech/M.Phil Computer Science scholars in the field of data mining, neural networks, bioinformatics, and application of Computer Science and IT in healthcare, disease diagnosis and prediction. She has had shorter stays at several Computing departments in China, UAE. Her research aptitude and acumen are of very high order.

♥♥♥

About the Editors

Satchidananda Dehuri (SMIEEE) is working as a Professor in the Department of Computer Science (Erstwhile Department of Information and Communication Technology), Fakir Mohan University, Balasore, Odisha, India since 2013. Prior to this appointment, for a short stint (i.e., from Oct. 2012 to May 2014) he was an Associate Professor in the Department of Systems Engineering, Ajou University, South Korea. He received his M.Tech. and Ph.D. degrees in Computer Science from Utkal University, Vani Vihar, Odisha in 2001 and 2006, respectively. He visited as a BOYSCAST Fellow to the Soft Computing Laboratory, Yonsei University, Seoul, South Korea under the BOYSCAST Fellowship Program of DST, Govt. of India in 2008. In 2010 he received Young Scientist Award in Engineering and Technology for the year 2008 from Odisha Vigyan Academy, Department of Science and Technology, Govt. of Odisha. In 2021 he received Teachers Associateship and Research Excellence (TARE) Fellowship from SERB, DST, Govt. of India for three years to carry out intensive research on Higher Order Neural Networks for Big Data Analysis at host Institute, ISI Kolkata and Parent Institute, Fakir Mohan University, Balasore. His research interests include Multi-objective Optimization, Machine Learning, and Data Science. He has already published 250 research papers in reputed journals and conference proceedings. Under his direct supervision, 20 PhD. Scholars have been successfully awarded in the area of Computer Science.

Index

A

aids, 105
algorithm, viii, ix, 1, 3, 6, 7, 8, 10, 11, 14, 15, 16, 22, 32, 34, 37, 39, 40, 42, 49, 52, 53, 54, 57, 67, 68, 69, 76, 79, 82, 83, 87, 89, 92, 94, 98, 99, 100, 103, 106, 107, 108, 118, 148, 153, 155, 157, 169
alignment, viii, 1, 2, 4, 5, 6, 7, 8, 9, 11, 13, 15
analysis, viii, ix, 31, 33, 34, 35, 43, 64, 65, 66, 68, 82, 85, 86, 88, 89, 90, 93, 100, 109, 113, 114, 116, 117, 118, 119, 121, 122, 123, 124, 125, 145, 149, 158, 176
anomaly, viii, 51, 52, 58, 64, 116
antenna, ix, 129, 130, 131, 132, 133, 134, 135, 137, 139, 140, 141, 144, 145, 146
architecture, 20, 56, 94, 96, 148, 153, 162, 173
automated, viii, 17, 20, 30, 52, 111

B

band gap, ix, 145
band notching, ix, 129, 144
Bangla, viii, 1, 2, 4, 5, 6, 11, 12, 13, 15
blockchain, ix, 161, 162, 164, 165, 166, 167, 168, 169, 170, 171, 172, 173, 174
blockchain-cloud, ix, 161, 166, 170, 171, 172, 173
blockchain-cloud healthcare models, 161

C

classification(s), viii, 22, 23, 30, 31, 40, 49, 54, 55, 58, 60, 65, 66, 67, 68, 69, 71, 74, 76, 78, 82, 83, 86, 87, 88, 89, 90, 103, 107, 108, 110, 111, 116, 118, 148, 158, 159
cloud, ix, 64, 161, 162, 163, 164, 165, 166, 167, 168, 169, 170, 172, 173, 174
communication(s), ix, 25, 29, 55, 63, 64, 88, 89, 90, 93, 121, 122, 123, 125, 129, 144, 145, 146, 152, 173, 175, 176
computer vision, 148, 152, 159
convolutional neural networks, ix, 107, 117, 147, 148, 153, 159
customer behavior, 113, 114

D

dataset, viii, 10, 17, 20, 29, 31, 33, 38, 39, 42, 43, 44, 53, 54, 56, 57, 58, 59, 60, 62, 63, 64, 65, 66, 68, 69, 70, 71, 75, 76, 77, 78, 81, 82, 83, 87, 90, 94, 96, 98, 102, 108, 114, 116, 121, 122, 148, 149, 153, 155, 156, 158
decision tree, viii, 40, 52, 56, 57, 58, 65, 66, 67, 68, 69, 70, 74, 75, 76, 82, 83, 87, 88, 89, 90, 116
deep learning, 18, 20, 22, 30, 34, 49, 64, 92, 117, 147, 148, 149, 151, 158, 159
deep neural networks, 92, 95, 100
detection, viii, 3, 17, 18, 20, 22, 25, 26, 27, 29, 30, 34, 51, 52, 53, 55, 56, 63, 64, 68, 89, 94, 100, 104, 105, 107, 116, 121, 149, 153, 154, 156, 159
diagnosis, 88, 89, 106, 109, 159, 162, 164, 175
digital, vii, 117, 121, 125, 148, 161, 162, 164

Index

digital healthcare system(s), 161, 162, 164
dimensionality reduction, 65, 66, 67, 76, 78, 81, 83
discriminant, 65, 68, 69, 76, 78, 81, 82, 88, 90
divergence, viii, 2, 3, 13
downlink, ix, 129, 144

E

electromagnetic, ix, 129, 130, 131, 134, 145, 146
electromagnetic band gaps (EBGs) structures, ix, 129, 130
estimation, viii, 1, 6, 7, 15, 52, 122
expectation, viii, 1, 2, 3, 16

F

face mask, viii, 17, 18, 20, 22, 26, 27, 29, 30
farm animal(s), ix, 101, 102, 104, 105, 109, 110

G

gain, 48, 55, 57, 70, 73, 74, 113, 130, 140, 141
gate, 26, 37
Gate, 37

H

hand gesture recognition, 148, 158, 159
healthcare system(s), ix, 105, 161, 162, 163, 164, 166, 172, 173
Highly Undetectable steGO (HUGO), 92, 94
hybrid, ix, 2, 49, 87, 89, 90, 161, 166, 173

I

integration, 170, 173
interoperable, 106, 110

K

keyless, 169, 173

L

least significant bit (LSB), ix, 92, 94, 100
limitation(s), 29, 55, 78, 81, 86, 87, 103, 166
linear discriminant analysis (LDA), viii, 65, 66, 69, 79, 80, 81, 82, 83, 84, 85, 86, 87, 88, 89, 90
livestock, 101, 102, 103, 104, 105, 107, 109, 110
LSTM-long short-term memory, 33

M

machine learning, ix, 1, 15, 18, 20, 22, 32, 33, 42, 48, 49, 51, 52, 59, 64, 66, 87, 88, 89, 90, 101, 102, 103, 104, 105, 106, 107, 108, 109, 110, 111, 114, 117, 148, 149, 151, 155, 158, 176
maximization, viii, 1, 2, 3, 14
motivation, 164

N

natural language processing, 114
neural networks, 30, 32, 35, 42, 43, 48, 49, 50, 64, 91, 92, 98, 99, 116, 125, 147, 153, 175, 176

O

Odia, viii, 1, 2, 3, 4, 5, 6, 12, 13, 14, 15
open loop slot & omni-directional, 130

P

prediction, viii, ix, 15, 31, 33, 34, 35, 37, 40, 45, 48, 49, 50, 52, 54, 56, 66, 68, 76, 87, 88, 89, 90, 98, 103, 105, 108, 111, 113, 148, 175

Index

principal component analysis (PCA), viii, 65, 66, 68, 76, 77, 78, 81, 82, 83, 84, 85, 86, 87, 89

probability, vii, 1, 2, 4, 5, 6, 7, 8, 9, 11, 12, 13, 14, 52, 70, 118

R

random forest classification, 33

random forest(s), viii, 31, 32, 33, 40, 45, 49, 51, 52, 53, 54, 56, 57, 58, 59, 60, 64, 108

return loss, 133, 139, 141, 142

S

safety, 17, 18, 19, 52, 94, 104

satellite(s), ix, 83, 129, 130, 144

security, 51, 52, 53, 63, 64, 92, 93, 104, 162, 164, 166, 167, 171, 172, 173

signature-based intrusion detection systems (SIDS), viii, 52

social media, ix, 113, 114, 116, 117, 121, 123, 125

steganography, ix, 91, 92, 93, 94, 95, 96, 97, 98, 99, 100

stock market, viii, 31, 32, 33, 34, 48, 49

stock market analysis, 33

supervised, ix, 3, 40, 54, 65, 101, 102, 103, 107, 109, 116

SVM-support vector machine, 33

T

temperature, viii, 17, 18, 20, 25, 26, 27, 29, 105, 108

trademark research data, 114

transliteration, 2, 4, 5

U

unsupervised, ix, 65, 101, 102, 103, 108, 116

UWB monopole antenna, 130, 146

V

vaccination, 26

W

wavelet obtained weights (WOW), 92